burning blue

D.M.W. GREER

burning blue

Oberon Books
London

First published by Oberon Books Ltd (incorporating
Absolute Classics), 521 Caledonian Road, London N7 9RH.
Tel: 0171 607 3637 / Fax: 0171 607 3629

British Library Cataloguing-in-Publication Data
A catalogue record for this book is available from the British Library.

ISBN 1 84002 024 5

Cover design: Andrzej Klimowski
Typography: Richard Doust

Printed in Great Britain by Arrowhead Books Ltd., Reading.

PREFACE

A seed falls into a crack in the middle of a six-lane highway. There's a bit of dirt, the sun shines, the rain falls, and regardless of the asphalt surrounding it, huge trucks rumbling past, that seed is going to grow. Although trapped in an utterly hostile environment it must follow the design nature has buried deep in its core – it must become what it is to become. This is the dilemma for the naval aviators in *burning blue*, who discover that the world in which they've invested all their hopes and dreams is completely at odds with the dictates of their hearts. We all make tough choices, but it's the rare individual who has the courage to give up everything – friends, family, career – to find out who he really is.

John Hickok

CHARACTERS

LT. DANIEL LYNCH IV: "Dano", 30ish, Navy F-18 fighter pilot. Annapolis graduate. Athletic, well-spoken, musical, quick to please. "All American". Son of an Admiral.

LT. WILL STEPHENSEN: "Wilbur", 30ish, Navy F-18 pilot. Annapolis graduate. Athletic, intelligent, competitive "guy's guy". Son of an Admiral. Dan's best friend.

SUSAN STEPHENSEN: 30ish, warm, attractive, well-educated wife of WILL. Mother of their son, Atticus.

LT. MATTHEW BLACKWOOD: "Iron Man", 30ish, Navy F-18 pilot. Annapolis graduate. Handsome, enigmatic, athletic "super hero". Son of a retired Admiral.

LT.j.g. CHARLIE TRUMBO: "Boner", 28, Navy F-18 pilot. Athletic, funny, painfully honest and unassuming. University of Arkansas graduate. Only child of pig farmers.

TAMMI BLACKWOOD: 30ish, acquisitive, "bubbly" Southern Baptist from Selma, Alabama. Wife of Matt Blackwood.

SPECIAL AGENT COKELY: 40ish, Naval Investigative Service (N.I.S.) Agent. Charming, cagey, seductive, psychotic.

SPECIAL AGENT JONES: 40ish, Black, Naval Investigative Service (N.I.S.) Agent. Abrasive, intuitive, oddly benevolent.

NANCY SPENCER 30ish, attractive, intelligent, loving. Estranged girlfriend of Dan.

Note: Tammi and Nancy can be played by the same Actress.

burning blue was first produced on London's Fringe at The King's Head Theatre in Islington on the 13th March 1995. It was directed by John Hickok with the following cast:

Lt. Dan Lynch, *Antony Edridge*

Lt. Will Stephensen, *Ian FitzGibbon*

Lt. Matt Blackwood, *Rob Bogue*

Lt.j.g. Charlie Trumbo, *Martin McDougall*

Susan Stephensen, *Katherine Hogarth*

Nancy Spencer/Tammi Blackwood, *Helene Kvale*

Special Agent Cokely, *David Pullan*

Special Agent Jones, *Basil Otion*

The play transferred to the West End's Theatre Royal, Haymarket on the 25th July 1995 with the following cast change:

Special Agent Cokely, *Tim Woodward*

Special Agent Jones, *Tony Armatrading*

It subsequently transferred to the Ambassador's Theatre on the 19th October 1995 where Nancy Spencer/Tammi Blackwood were played by *Elizabeth Perry*. Since then there have been productions in South Africa (1996), Tel Aviv (1997), Los Angeles and New York (1998).

High Flight

Oh! I have slipped the surly bonds of earth
And danced the skies on laughter-silvered wings;
Sunward I've climbed, and joined the tumbling mirth
Of sun-split clouds and done a hundred things
You have not dreamed of – wheeled and soared and swung
High in the sunlit silence. Hov'ring there,
I've chased the shouting wind along, and flung
My eager craft through footless halls of air.
Up, up the long, delirious burning blue
I've topped the wind-swept heights with easy grace
Where never Lark, or even Eagle flew –
And while with silent lifting mind I've trod
The high untrespassed sanctity of space,
Put out my hand and touched the face of God.

John Gillespie Magee, Jr.

The action takes place in a series of locations and scenes which shift rapidly between the present and the past:

the shoreline of Pensacola Bay; an Interrogation Room at the Pentagon; a Hotel Room in Philadelphia; a Discotheque in Hong Kong; a Stateroom aboard the nuclear-powered aircraft carrier Harry S. Truman; the Signal Bridge of the Truman; the VFA-133 Hangar at Naval Air Station Alameda, California; Will and Susan's Quarters at N.A.S. Alameda; Arlington National Cemetary; Dan's Apartment in San Francisco; Dan's Temporary Bachelor Officer's Quarters in Arlington, Virginia; a Hotel Room in Arlington.

PROLOGUE

In the blackout we hear two small explosions and see a flash of light. A few moments later we hear a popping sound as two parachutes snap open. In half-light a white parachute settles on the stage. Night time. The shoreline of Pensacola Bay. Lt. DAN LYNCH, 30, a Navy fighter pilot, struggles to free himself from his torso harness; his parachute is caught in the trees. Meanwhile his co-pilot, Lt. WILL STEPHENSEN, splashes into the water a few feet from shore. The parachute covers him.

DAN: Wilbur? Wilbur!

We hear coughing as a panicked WILL gasps for air. DAN continues to struggle with his harness so he can get to his buddy.

WILL: Dano... I can't breath... I can't breath! Dano?! Danoooooo!

At last freeing himself, DANO rushes offstage into the water and pulls WILL the short distance to shore. He frees his head from the parachute and we see his face covered in blood. DAN tries to calm him as WILL continues to panic.

WILL: Oh, God! Oh, my God! I'm bleeding... I'm bleeding!

DAN: You're fine, buddy. You're doing fine...

WILL: Where am I bleeding from?!

DAN: I told you, Will, you're okay!

WILL: My legs! I lost one of my legs, didn't I?!

DAN: Just calm down, Wilbur! You're gonna be fine!

WILL: (*Looking at his hands.*) Mother fuck... my brains... my brains are all over my hands!!

DAN: (*Shaking him.*) Just shut up for a minute! You've got to calm down and listen to me! A bird came through the canopy and hit you in the face. It's bird blood and bird guts.

WILL: Birds? I didn't see any birds... where are we, Dano?!

DAN: Somewhere on the shore of Pensacola Bay.

WILL: I'm freezing...

DAN: Take nice easy breaths and relax.

WILL: I'm so cold.

DAN: (*Cupping his hands for him.*) Here, blow into your hands...

WILL: I thought I was drowning... I thought I was gonna go straight to the bottom.

DAN: You were only ten feet from shore you wouldn't have drowned in three feet of water... no way.

DAN wipes the blood off WILL's hands and then takes hold of his feet.

WILL: Aghhhh! Jesus, that hurts! What are you doing?

DAN: I'm gonna get you warm by blowing on your feet. Now just lie back and concentrate on breathing slowly.

WILL: Go easy! I think my ankle's broken.

DAN: Nah... (*Looking at it suspiciously.*) It's probably just a bad sprain.

WILL: What about you, Dano, are you okay?

DAN: I'm fine, buddy, just lie back and take it easy.

WILL lies back partially while DAN bandages his ankle.

WILL: (*Anguished.*) It's over... it's over... my career's over. A week away from getting our wings and I went and fucked us both!

DAN: It's not over! A bird strike can happen to anybody.

WILL: (*Sitting up and clutching DAN's chest.*) Dano- I... I forgot to lock my visor down... the clouds came in and it got dark so fast- I couldn't see- so I raised my helmet visor and... I broke the regs! What if they find out I was flying with my visor up?

DAN: They won't. Don't worry...

WILL: But there's gonna be an Accident Investigation! I'm fucked... completely fucked!

WILL breaks down. After a beat, DAN gets up and smashes his own helmet visor.

WILL: What are you doing?

DAN: From now on I had command of the plane! The story is... we landed at one of the abandoned fields and... I moved into the front seat. We took off and... the birds came through the canopy shattering my visor and then we ejected. Got it?

WILL: But what if they find my helmet in the bay? They're gonna know I didn't have my visor secured down.

DAN: Just– just tell 'em you raised it after you hit the water.

WILL: If we lie and they find out we're both history!

DAN: What are you gonna do if you can't fly? Sell widgets in Omaha? No way! We've come too far! We're *both* getting our wings next week, Wilbur! We started together and that's the way we're gonna finish!
DAN wraps WILL's feet in the parachute and goes back to WILL and cradles him.

WILL: I just scuttled a twenty million dollar aircraft...

DAN: No way, that airframe was a piece of junk! I'm surprised the seats fired.
They huddle up together and are quiet for a few beats. DAN begins to laugh.

WILL: What's so freakin' funny?

DAN: (*He rubs his butt.*) Nothing like a rocket under your ass to shake up your world. (*He's quiet for a moment and then begins to laugh again.*) We must've looked like a couple of Roman Candles up there!

WILL: I don't find this humorous, Dano, pilots with accidents on their records aren't selected for NASA... this is serious shit! Your dad is gonna have your balls.
DAN hates hearing this.

DAN: A flock of birds fouled the engine! What could we do!? Whether your visor was up or down doesn't change the fact that we had to abandon the aircraft! And you! You initiated a text-book ejection!

WILL: Me? You mean you.

DAN: No. *You*... remember? Hell, they'll probably give you a medal!

WILL looks at DAN and suddenly freezes.

DAN: What? What is it?

WILL leans forward tentatively and wipes what looks like a bloody gash near DAN's eye.

WILL: (*He pretends to taste his finger.*) ... Gooney Bird.

DAN pushes him playfully and they fall in a heap laughing wildly.

WILL: Our aircraft is a junk heap at the bottom of Mobile Bay... but we made it! We got out! Cuz we're shit-hot!

DAN: Damn straight! (*He hugs WILL.*) We're alive! So... fuck 'em!

WILL: Yeah! Fuck 'em if they can't take a joke!!

Blackout.

ACT I

Scene 1

Five years later. An Interrogation Room at the Pentagon. Two Naval Investigative Service (N.I.S.) agents, COKELY and JONES, are reviewing a Service Record beside a table and chair. JONES seems tired, agitated.

JONES: Come on, John, everybody's got skeletons. I don't think he's told us what really happened.

COKELY: It's all here in the accident report. It was a bird strike, a Gooney Bird shattered the canopy. The board said it wasn't their fault (*Checking the record.*) they received their Aviators Wings eight days later. Case closed.

JONES: A bird? You really believe that?

COKELY: Have you ever seen what a deer can do to a car? It's the same thing in the air.

JONES: (*Reading.*) Stephensen had multiple lacerations to the face and a fractured ankle... Lynch was... in the front seat and was... uninjured? That's strange.

COKELY: Strange? Why?

JONES: I don't know... (*Tired. Squeezing his brow.*) Maybe it isn't. Let's just...

COKELY: (*Reading.*) The Search and Rescue team didn't find them till early the next morning.

JONES: (*Checking his watch impatiently.*) C'mon, let's stick to the case at hand, John...

COKELY: He *is* acting strange. You think he's hiding something?

JONES: Well he did just bury one of his buddies this afternoon. What was his name?

COKELY: (*Consulting another file.*) Blackwood... Matthew. Why?

JONES: Nothin'. Look, I've been up since...

COKELY: (*Reading the file.*) Jesus, Blackwood's Old Man was an Admiral too... Chief of Naval Personnel before he retired. You can bet he's livin' the good life now... in some huge mansion on a golf course... with a pool in the backyard.

JONES: Yeah, so what of it?

COKELY: I grew up with guys like Blackwood and Lynch.

JONES: You did?

COKELY: Yeah, my Old Man was an Officer... I know what makes 'em tick.

JONES: Good for you, John, a quiet evening with my wife makes me tick. I'm gonna get straight to the point with...

COKELY: I'm not gonna shotgun this interview and risk damaging his career just cuz you've had a long day! Remember, his old man is a four-star...

JONES: You don't need to remind me. I'm very aware of that. I just wish you'd gotten the informant's name. (*Looking at the file.*) One telephone call from Hong Kong... from a source you've never even met much less done a background check on?

COKELY: Trust me. He was legit, he knew too much about it not to be. If we nip this thing in the bud, it'll save the Navy from a lot of embarrassing publicity and it'll save both the Lieutenant's and the Admiral's careers. His old man will be kissin' our feet. Now, we have to get as much information from him as possible...

JONES: John– I've been doing this for years, I know the drill by...

As JONES is talking, DAN enters wearing his Service Dress Blues with hat in hand.

COKELY: Everything squared away, Lieutenant?

DAN: Yes, Sir. I've secured a seat on a commercial flight back to San Francisco tonight.

COKELY: Excellent. Now... somehow we skipped the beginning of the interview when we started talking

about that little mishap in Pensacola a few years back.
(*Looking at DAN's record again.*) The "F" stands for?

DAN: Forsythe. Daniel Forsythe Lynch, the fourth.

JONES: (*Taking the record from COKELY.*) You graduated
eleventh out of 950... I thought all the Lynch's finished
first in their class?

DAN: (*Embarrassed.*) Actually, sir, I think that's a typo...
it should be a one.

JONES: (*Glaring at him.*) For the record Lieutenant, would
you give us your Social Security number and duty
station?

DAN: (*Confused, tentative.*) 113-45-6737. I'm stationed with
VFA-133 (one-thirty-three) out of Alameda, California.

JONES: (*Increasingly brusque.*) Have you ever gone by any
other name, Lieutenant?

DAN: Sir?

JONES: Special Agent Jones is fine. Have you ever used
any other name?

DAN: Any other name?

COKELY: (*Stepping in to defuse JONES.*) This isn't a trick
question. Just relax, Dan.

JONES: (*Impatiently.*) Yes or no?

DAN: (*Turning to COKELY.*) Sir, I was under the impression
I'd been called in here to answer questions regarding–
I'm not tracking.

COKELY: (*Extending his hand.*) Special Agent Cokely.
Please, call me John. I thought we'd introduced ourselves
earlier up at Arlington Cemetary. Pardon me if we didn't
explain the procedure here. It's just a routine question all
Naval Investigative Service agents ask. No big deal. Have
you ever gone by any other name?

DAN: Well... my friends and family call me Dano, or Danny
and... oh yeah... my grandparents called me Ivey.

JONES: "Ivey"?

DAN: You know, "I" and "V"? It comes from the Roman
numerals one and five at the end of my name. It's a

southern nickname for fourth generation sons. *(The agents watch DAN as he thinks.)* My brother calls me "Dan Dan".

COKELY: "Dan Dan"?

DAN: Yes, sir. *(Chuckling.)* Sounds like a character from the Flintstones doesn't it? That's my younger brother, Dylan, who calls me "Dan Dan". He's younger... much...

JONES: *(Icily.)* We meant your last name. Does your wife call you "Dan Dan" also?

DAN: I'm not married.

COKELY: Oh? *(He glances at JONES.)* That wasn't your wife we saw at the funeral...?

JONES: What does your girlfriend call you?

DAN: *(With a nervous laugh.)* Anything but late for dinner.

COKELY: I'm sure you let her call you anything her little heart desires.

DAN: I guess so.

COKELY: And what is her name?

DAN: Nancy.

COKELY: Well, you're a lucky man.

DAN: *(Realizing COKELY is mistaken.)* Oh, no. That wasn't Nancy you saw today that was Susan. Nancy is back in San Francisco. She... couldn't make it out.

JONES: *(To COKELY.)* We're talking to "Don Juan" with the alias Dan Lynch.

COKELY: Girl in every port?

DAN: Not exactly. Susan is Will Stephensen's wife.

COKELY: *(Glancing at JONES.)* Who's Will Stephensen?

DAN: A close friend. He's also a pilot in VFA-133.

JONES: How close?

DAN: I'd say he's my best friend.

JONES: Like best buddies?

DAN: Yes. He and I and– Lt. Blackwood... were classmates at the Academy.

Crossfade to

Scene 2

Seven years before the interrogation. A hotel room in Philadelphia after the Army/Navy game. WILL and MATT enter arm-in-arm singing. They pull DAN up out of the previous scene and drape a Bridge Coat over his shoulder. WILL has lost his clothes in a bet so he's wearing only boxers and a t-shirt under his Bridge Coat. MATT is wearing his Service Dress Blues under his Bridge Coat. They pass a flask back and forth.

ALL: WE DON'T PLAY NOTRE DAME... WE DON'T PLAY TULAAAANE... WE JUST PLAY HOLY CROSS CUZ THAT'S THE FEARLESS ARMY WAY!

They stumble around the room arm-in-arm laughing and singing. Suddenly they see the bed located offstage beyond the fourth wall.

DAN: Only one single bed?

WILL: (*Giving him a tiny twister.*) You'll grow to like it.

MATT: Hey, wait a minute, I asked for a room with two doubles and a roll-away. I want a refund!

MATT begins adjusting the radio as he picks up the house phone.

DAN: And I gotta take a piss. (*He exits stage right.*)

WILL: Like a racehorse!

MATT: Yes, Ma'am, this is Midshipman *First Class* Blackwood in room Eight fourteen...

WILL: Watch out! Mattie's pullin' rank.

MATT: Hello? (*To them.*) She put me on hold.

DAN: (*Still offstage.*) I've got something she can hold!

WILL: I was leaving the men's room at halftime and some Army 'Whoop' taps me on the shoulder and says "At West Point they teach us to wash our hands after we take a piss"...

DAN: (*Emptying the flask.*) You're fuckin' kiddin' me?!

WILL: Swear to God.

DAN: I would've hauled off and leveled the geek. What'd you do?

WILL: I told him "At Annapolis..."

MATT: (*Stealing the joke.*) "They teach us not to piss on our hands"!!

WILL: Eat my shorts, Iron Man! I had him on that one.

MATT finds a classical station and conducts passionately. WILL watches intently for a moment and then turns to DAN entering from the bathroom.

WILL: (*To MATT.*) Hey, change the station, you got the wrong city for the pops... were in Philie, dude!

DAN: For the last time! Our fourth... and last... Army/Navy game!

WILL: YeeeeeHAW! Next year we'll be in Pensacola doin' what every civilian swingin' dick can only dream about!

MATT: Yeah! We're fuckin' outta here! (*Into the phone.*) I didn't mean here... excuse me, Ma'am. Yes, this is Midshipman Blackwood in room eight-fourteen, I reserved a room with two doubles and a roll-away like we had for last year's Army/Navy game but the room we were given has only one single bed...

MATT continues explaining the problem. DAN jumps up and is wheeling the T.V. downstage toward an imaginary window. WILL joins him.

DAN: Tell her if she doesn't give us the room we reserved the T.V. goes out the window!

WILL: No!! Tell her we'll make a deal! She sends up a bartender and some Glenlivet and we'll forget about the bigger room!

DAN: (*They're both hugging the television.*) Otherwise the Zenith goes out the window!

MATT: (*Covering the phone.*) Along with our commissions! Shut the fuck up, I have the situation under control. (*He listens.*) Yes, Ma'am? No problem... Thank you. (*He hangs up.*) She's *deeply* sorry for the mixup there are no more rooms with double beds available.

DAN and WILL pick up the T.V. prepared to throw it out the window. MATT forces it back on the ground. A huge grin crosses his face.

MATT: However, the Porter will be up momentarily to help us move to our *suite* with two *king* size beds... and a roll-away for Wilbur... compliments of the hotel.

DAN: You're shittin' me? How'd that happen?

WILL: We fall into a pile of dog shit and within minutes we're smellin' like a rose! You freakin' amaze me, dude!

MATT changes the station and "Can't Take My Eyes Off of You" by Vikki Carr comes on the radio. WILL grabs DAN around the waist and starts doing the Can-Can.

WILL: "I LOVE YOU BAABY... AND IF ITS QUITE ALRIGHT..."

WILL: (*To MATT.*) C'mon let your hair down, buddy! We don't have to be back in Annapolis until seventeen hundred tomorrow... you're makin' me feel like a freakin' lush.

DAN: Come on, Matt, you've drunk twice as much as Wilbur and me you should be able to kick twice as high!

DAN and WILL are arm-in-arm. WILL tries to pull MATT to his side but he remains seated.

DAN: "I NEED YOU BABY ALL THROUGH THE LONELY NIGHT..."

ALL: "TRUST IN ME WHEN I SAAAY... OHH PRETTY BAABY..."

WILL: I'm gonna be the first man to walk on Mars!

MATT: Walk? (*He holds up the flask.*) I'm gonna run its circumference!

WILL: In my tracks, Iron Man! I'll run you and those Martians into the dust!

MATT: Just like we ran all over Army today... right, Wilbur?

WILL: If only they hadn't made that extra point!

DAN: Yeah... we would have won the game!!

WILL: And I'd still have my clothes!

DAN: Come on, Mattie, get your ass up here!

MATT: I don't dance, dude.

WILL & DAN: Oh yes you do!

> *They pull MATT up out of the chair and put him in the middle of a kick line. Within seconds they're kicking in unison as they sing with the radio.*

ALL: "DAADA, DAADA, DAADA, DADA–DA–DAADA, DADA DAAAAAHH–I LOVE YOU BABY..."

> *WILL and MATT remove DAN's coat and exit. DAN returns to the interrogation.*
>
> *Crossfade to*

Scene 3

> *The present. The Interrogation Room. The Agents are standing. DAN is still seated.*

JONES: *Third* in Primary Right Training?

DAN: Stiff competition, sir.

JONES: Who beat you to those number one and two positions, Lieutenant?

DAN: Lieutenants Blackwood and Stephensen. (*Seeking refuge from COKELY.*) I don't mean to be disrespectful, Special Agent Cokely but–

COKELY: Call me John. Please.

DAN: Yes, sir. Why are we talking about my Service Record and the bird strike in Pensacola five years ago. I thought I was here to answer questions pertaining to last Monday's accident.

JONES: (*Looking at COKELY.*) Did we say that? Why do you think you're here, Don?

DAN: Dan.

JONES: Whatever. Any ideas?

DAN: You seem to be curious about Susan and Will.

JONES: Perhaps.

> *DAN is growing visibly nervous.*

COKELY: Lieutenant?

DAN: (*Distracted.*) Yes, sir?

COKELY: Dan? (*Getting his attention.*) Tell us about your port call in Hong Kong last month. I'm curious about August the 13th.

DAN: August 13th? (*Hesitant.*) I was aboard the Truman in Hong Kong Harbor. The ship had pulled in for a couple days of liberty before steaming home to San Francisco.

They all exit.

Crossfade to

Scene 4

Four weeks earlier. A four-man Stateroom aboard the nuclear -powered aircraft carrier HARRY S. TRUMAN. We see two sets of bunkbeds perpendicular to one another with lockers attached to the ends and a desk in between. Two naval aviators, Lt.j.g. CHARLIE TRUMBO and Lt. WILL STEPHENSEN, F-18 pilots, enter out of breath from running.

CHARLIE: I'll be the first one to admit you can kick my butt in the cross-country department any day of the week.

WILL: Damn straight, Boner, now you're starting to speak the truth.

CHARLIE: But then again, you've been trainin' with Dan Lynch and Matt Blackwood since God was a child. How many marathons have you run?

WILL: Only two. Matt's the dude that takes leave in Hawaii every year to run the "Iron Man".

CHARLIE: Amazin'... he was up partyin' all night long in Hong Kong, gets maybe an hour of sleep and then runs consecutive six-minute miles around a boilin' hot flight deck in the middle of the afternoon.

WILL: Oh, so you were with Iron Man and Dano last night too? Thanks a shitload for bilging me.

CHARLIE: I didn't bilge you, Wilbur.

WILL: You just said you were out all night with...

CHARLIE: I spent most of the night at the Peninsula Hotel drinking with two other nuggets from fifty-three.

WILL: Dano and I'd made plans. I blew my whole evening waiting for that dirt-bag. How many times you get laid?

CHARLIE: None.

WILL: Now I know you're feeding me a line.

CHARLIE: I'm tellin' you the truth, I rented a room at the Peninsula with some guys from fifty-three.

WILL: Don't tell me you're going queer on me.

CHARLIE: We did have two Navy Nurses with us.

WILL: AHA! See, I knew you got laid, you son-of-a-bitch!

CHARLIE: No, I don't think I did.

WILL: You don't *think* you did?

CHARLIE: I mean, I'm almost certain I didn't... I was pretty blasted. I do remember the other guys were taking turns doin' one of the nurses while...

WILL: You're unfuckinbelievable, Boner! A second ago you're telling me you didn't get laid and now I find out it was a freakin' orgy with the entire Navy Nurse Corps.

CHARLIE: Honestly, I'm pretty certain I didn't dip my wick.

WILL: Well, let me see if I can help you recall. Were your clothes off?

CHARLIE: (*Thinking.*) Yes...

WILL: Before you brushed this morning, did your mouth taste like an old penny?

CHARLIE: Hmm? I suppose so, but–

WILL: Case closed.

CHARLIE: Circumstantial evidence! I remember I was trying to console one of the ladies while the other guys were jackhammerin' her friend in the bedroom. See she was all upset and feelin' guilty on account of she'd only ever been with...

WILL: Where the hell was Dano?

CHARLIE: I'm assumin' he and Iron Man partied all night long.

DAN and MATT quietly enter from the showers wrapped in towels.

WILL: That dude's a freakin' machine. Next Air Combat Maneuver I'm gonna make sure Matt's my bogey and hand his ass to him on a platter.

CHARLIE: How you gonna do that, Wilbur? Iron Man's never lost an ACM... he's untouchable.

WILL: (*He snaps a towel at CHARLIE's crotch.*) Hey, kiss my grits, Boner.

MATT: Whose ass are you gonna be serving on a platter, Will?

WILL: (*Startled, he turns.*) Yours if there isn't any hot water left!

DAN: Hot water? (*Officially.*) "The big Harry has not one but *two* state-of-the-art nuclear reactors capable of providing unlimited hot water for a crew of 6,000 for the next 15 years."

CHARLIE: Endless supplies of hot H2O. God bless the atom!

Just as MATT and DAN remove their towels, the lights go out and then come back up to a deep red. The following few lines are delivered rapidly; almost in unison.

MATT: What the...

DAN: Son of a bitch!

CHARLIE: I didn't hear anyone announce darken-ship.

WILL: Darken-ship?! We're pulling out of Hong Kong Harbor in the middle of the afternoon. Guess the Executive Officer is trying to keep the crew on their toes.

MATT: No, Wilbur, he's screwing with the Air Wing... not the crew. Have you seen him in his khakis lately? Ten pounds of shit in a five pound bag!

WILL: Just another angry four-eyed, lard-ass, black-shoe!

MATT: He's just smart enough to know he's only a chauffeur...

ALL: (*They high five each other.*) For Aviators!

WILL: Classic "Napoleon Complex"...

MATT: Of fat asses...

DAN: Yeah, the "four-eyed, fucked-up, fat-ass complex."

WILL: Speaking of fucked-up, where were you two dirtbags last night?

This momentarily throws both DAN and MATT. They steal a glance at each other.

DAN: Uh... we lost track of time. Sorry, Wilbur. It wasn't intentional.

WILL: No big deal... I just blew my only night off in two months.

DAN: I'm sorry. I really am.

CHARLIE: Hey, fellas, we're pullin' outta here in less than an hour.

WILL: I'm headed for the showers.

CHARLIE: Right behind you.

WILL: Hey, Dano, where's your shampoo?

DAN: There on the desk.

WILL gropes around in the half-light unable to distinguish which is the shampoo bottle.

WILL: Where?

DAN: Right in front of your eyes, Wilbur.

CHARLIE grabs WILL's hand and puts his penis in it.

CHARLIE: Here ya go big guy... just squeeze and apply to scalp.

WILL: Whoa! You are one sick fuck!

They head for the exit with towels around their waists.

DAN: Check your six o'clock position, Will, he's right behind you. He didn't get the name "Boner" for nothing!

WILL and CHARLIE exit. The lights come back to normal. DAN and MATT continue to dress in their Service Dress Blues. An awkward beat.

MATT: Dress Blues?

DAN: Yeah. Dinner with my dad in the Flag Mess. He must've forgotten his whites.

MATT: Eighty-five degrees... ninety percent humidity... a dozen men in winter uniform.

DAN: "Rank hath its privileges."

MATT: (*Mimicking Rod Sterling.*) Until twenty-two hundred hours, you will cease to exist as Dan Lynch... you'll be "Admiral Lynch's son"... son of the Commander in Chief of the Pacific Fleet...

DAN: Son of the biggest sonofabitch in the United States Navy.

MATT: Known by none... feared by all. (*Facetiously.*) Except his son, of course. "Yay, as we walk in the shadow of our father's careers... we will watch our step... for their egos and their power will always eclipse ours."

DAN smiles then suddenly he hobbles over to the chair grabbing his calf in pain. MATT ministers to him immediately attempting to knead out a cramp.

DAN: Shit. Shit. Damn that hurts!

MATT: I told you to stretch out more after you finish a long run, Bozo!

DAN grits his teeth. After several beats the pain begins to subside.

DAN: Thanks. That's better.

MATT: (*Still kneading it.*) You've got to get the lactic acid out or it'll cramp up again.

Suddenly MATT stops, aware of DAN's proximity. He moves to the other side of the room and continues dressing. After a beat, DAN continues dressing and finally breaks the awkward silence.

DAN: We must've been keeping about a seven minute pace up there.

MATT: Yeah.

DAN: Boner did well, considering he never runs.

Uncomfortable pause. MATT picks up his synthesized guitar.

MATT: Yeah. Not bad for a farm boy. (*Playing with the tape replay.*) Dammit, Charlie!

27

DAN: What?

MATT: Boner's been in my shit.

DAN: Boner wouldn't mess with– (*Suddenly noticing.*) That was me, Matt...

MATT: What the fuck were you–? Forget it.

DAN: I'm sorry... I guess my curiousity got the best of me. I didn't know that thing could sound like so many instruments. (*No response.*) Hey, I didn't mean to–

MATT: I said forget it.

> *Uncomfortable pause. DAN walks to the other side of the room.*

DAN: I'd like to hear more.

MATT: Yeah?

DAN: Yeah. Remember last night when you said you wanted me to hear the instrumental piece you've been working on? I thought–

MATT: Last night was a mistake! I shouldn't have said anything. (*Softening.*) It's a work in progress.

> *Crossfade to*

Scene 5

The present. The Interrogation Room.

COKELY: (*Looking at his notes.*) You and Lt. Blackwood spent the evening touring Hong Kong and then drank beers at a streetside cafe before returning to the ship about 0500 the next morning... August the 14th.

DAN: Yes, sir.

JONES: What were you doing until 5 a.m., Lieutenant?

DAN: Like I said, drinking beer.

JONES: Did you drink the city dry?

DAN: Guess we had quite a bit.

JONES: (*He looks at COKELY then at DAN.*) Now... enough cat and mouse, Dan. You parted company with Lt. Blackwood and ventured off to a night club didn't you?

DAN: Sir?

JONES: Do you remember what that night club was called?

DAN: (*Nervously nonchalant.*) There must be dozens of–

JONES: You don't remember it was called... "Disco-Disco"?

DAN: You know Hong Kong, the back streets are jammed with night clubs. We probably checked out several.

JONES: But you did go to a club called "Disco-Disco", correct?

DAN: If you say so. I told you, we'd had a few beers.

JONES: You didn't notice anything unusual about "Disco-Disco"? That it was a "special" kind of night club?

DAN: It seemed like any other disco to me. When you've been drinking they all seem–

JONES: You didn't notice this one had a rather special clientele!?

DAN: (*Nervously.*) Not particularly.

JONES stares DAN down for several beats, then turns and whispers with COKELY. They confer and then refer to his record. This takes several moments. DAN sweats.

JONES: You didn't notice, Lieutenant, that it was... a homosexual night club?

DAN: (*Stunned and grasping for an answer.*) Sir, Matt Blackwood and I were together the entire evening. If he were here he'd confirm–

JONES: Don't lie to us, Lieutenant!!

COKELY: (*To JONES.*) Hey, go easy, Jonesie! (*Apologetically.*) Listen, Dan, we received a report that you were seen engaged in a homosexual act.

Startled, DAN jerks to attention. He rapidly scans JONES and COKELY.

DAN: What?!

COKELY: It was probably some vindictive "jar-head" Marine trying to get back at you for denying him a liberty request or something. Special Agent Jones and I field accusations like this pretty regularly and most of them, as I'm sure this one is, are unfounded. But, given who your father is... and your visibility... we have to get to the bottom of this ASAP. I'm here to help prove your innocence. You are innocent?

DAN: Yes, sir.

JONES: (*Derisively.*) There must be someone from the ship that saw you with Blackwood at the outdoor cafe, what about your friend, Lt. Stephensen?

DAN: No. Like I said, we lost track of time... we forgot to meet him.

COKELY: Can he vouch for you? On your character in general?

DAN: He must know me better than– I'd appreciate it if you'd keep him out of this.

COKELY and JONES realize DAN has just unwittingly implicated himself.

COKELY: Of course. (*He looks at JONES conspiratorially and then at his watch.*) Eight o'clock already. Tell you what, Dan, why don't you take a Head Call and I'll run out and pick us up some sandwiches for dinner.

DAN: Sir, my return flight leaves at 2115... the ship sails in less than 48 hours... I really need to get back to–

COKELY: Don't worry, we'll get you out on the first hop tomorrow morning. Now, why don't we all take a break?

JONES: That means you, Lieutenant. I wouldn't pass up this opportunity.

Rattled, DAN stands, buttons his jacket and begins to exit for the men's room.

COKELY: Say, Dan! Ham and cheese good for you?

DAN: Fine. Thank you. (*He exits.*)

JONES: The guy went to a gay bar but that doesn't...

COKELY is putting on his jacket and preparing to exit.

JONES: Where the hell are you going?

COKELY: Naval Air Station Alameda, California to interview his other friends.

JONES: Alameda?! You expect me to hang out here while you go hunt for homos in San Francisco?

COKELY: Calm down, Jonesie, I'll be back tomorrow afternoon. Now don't wimp out on me, we're gonna need as much information as possible to save him.

JONES: Since when did you–? He'll ask where you went. (*No answer.*) What about dinner?!

COKELY: Tell him the local deli was out of ham and cheese and I'm checking all the others in the area.

Blackout.

Scene 6

Very early the next morning. A squadron hangar at Naval Air Station Alameda, California. WILL holds his flight helmet in one hand and adjusts his G-suit on his way out to his plane.

COKELY: Lt. Stephensen?

WILL: Yes?

COKELY: As in Adlai?

WILL: No. As in "PH" and "E" in place of a "V" and an "0".

COKELY: (*Reviewing his notes.*) Last week was your second ejection in five years. Let's see... the first time you suffered... a compound fracture of the ankle and... this time? How's your head?

WILL: Just a few knocks. I'm fine. Who are you?

COKELY: John Cokely, N.I.S.. I just need you to answer a few questions. (*Scribbling into a notepad.*) Your date of birth is?

WILL: 9-1-59. Questions about what?

COKELY: Well, happy belated birthday, Lieutenant.

WILL: (*Pause.*) Thanks.

COKELY: Did you celebrate?

WILL: My wife and I had a few friends over for dinner...

COKELY: Susan, right?

WILL: Have you met?

31

COKELY: Any children?

WILL: A son. Atticus. He was christened last Saturday.

COKELY: Now, Will... do you mind if I call you Will?

WILL: (*Reluctantly.*) That's fine.

COKELY: Will, I've been reviewing your Service Record and the Accident Report from your Pensacola punch-out a few years ago... now it seems to me– Let's get right down to it, Will. I understand you and Lt. Lynch have a special friendship... a little secret. Can you elaborate on that for me?

WILL grows nervous.

COKELY: Will?

WILL: I'm sorry, I don't understand.

COKELY: What's to understand?

WILL starts to sweat. He believe COKELY's found out about the cover up from years before.

COKELY: Will... is there something you'd like to tell me... something you and Lt. Lynch have been hiding?

WILL: What do you mean?

COKELY: I think you know.

WILL: Do I?

COKELY: Would you prefer we talk to your father about this?

WILL: You haven't spoken to him, have you?

COKELY: Not yet.

WILL: And my skipper?

COKELY: I talk to a lot of people. Look, Will, I'm the one that's supposed to be asking the questions.

WILL: Have you spoken to my Squadron Commander?

COKELY: Last month, August the 13th, the night before your ship left Hong Kong, where did you and Lt. Lynch go that night?

WILL: (*Confused.*) What?

COKELY: August 13th. Tell me where you went with Lynch.

WILL: I never even saw Dan during that Port Call.

COKELY: No? When did you next see him?

WILL: We ran a few miles around the deck of the carrier and then shot the breeze up on the Signal Bridge after steaming out of Hong Kong. Why?

COKELY: Just the two of you?

Crossfade to

Scene 7

A month earlier. The sun is setting in the middle of the Pacific Ocean. Occasionally we hear the sound of a jet passing overhead. MATT and WILL stand on the Signal Bridge of the aircraft carrier, the highest location on the ship, and salute as they watch DAN's dad arrive below.

WILL: I just need a couple of weeks... three max. Until the T.P.S. billets are assigned.

MATT: Skipper's gonna wonder why you're not on the night Flight Schedule.

WILL: It's just a minor eye infection... nothing serious.

We hear a bosun's whistle and they drop their salute.

MATT: Maybe you should see the Doc, Will...

WILL: I can't. C'mon, Iron Man, just help me with–

Suddenly MATT sees DAN arrive from behind WILL. WILL abruptly stops and turns.

WILL: Dano! Hey! I'm... gonna run below and get that press release for you to look at.

DAN: Okay. Sure.

WILL exits. An awkward beat. They both look out.

MATT: How's the cramp?

DAN: Fine.

MATT: Skipper asked where I went last night.

DAN: (*Pause.*) Do you think one of the women called the ship?

MATT: You didn't say anything to him, did you?

DAN: Absolutely not.

MATT: Good. Loose lips sink ships. (*With difficulty.*)
    I need some professional advice.

DAN: You can talk to me, Matt.

MATT: You can't be objective.

DAN: Why not?

MATT: You like my music too much.

   *DAN and MATT exchange glances. MATT tries to suppress a
   smile.*

MATT: You didn't tell Wilbur where we went, did you?

DAN: No... but I plan to.

   *DAN lifts the camera from his neck and snaps a photo of the
   ocean.*

MATT: Hold off awhile.

DAN: (*Cautiously.*) Do you care about her?

MATT: Tammi? Sure. It may not be perfect but– (*Pause.*)
    Tammi is good for me.

DAN: Who are you trying to convince?

MATT: (*In a stage whisper.*) Hey, I didn't plan this! I'm not
    interested in living my life like a freak. Fairies, guys in
    leather, drag queens– I have nothing in common with
    them.

DAN: Neither do I! (*A sudden revelation.*) Actually, I do. The
    last few times Nancy and I had sex... I closed my eyes...
    and all I saw was you.

MATT: You're better than that, you can rise above it!

DAN: Above what?

MATT: This... infatuation.

DAN: Infatuation? (*Incredulously.*) Do you remember how
    you looked at me last night? When we were on the
    launch headed back to the ship? I do.

MATT: This discussion is over!

DAN: You initiated this whole thing.

MATT: I was trashed, I shouldn't have said anything.

DAN: So was I. You asked me a question. I answered it.

MATT: I don't remember who asked whom.

DAN: Have some conviction, Matt, don't blame it on the beer! You're the one that suggested we go with that Chinese girl to the disco.

MATT: We were in Hong Kong– it was a fucking costume party.

DAN: If only I'd had my camera. I've never seen you have so much fun.

MATT: (*Signals with stiff hand across his throat.*) Cut it!

DAN: Don't worry, I'm off to T.P.S. after this cruise anyway. (*No response.*) Why are you wearing Dress Blues?

MATT: Chaplain asked me to join him for dinner in the Flag Mess. Probably with your father.

DAN: I'll try not to let my dad catch me whistling in your direction.

MATT: Fuck you, Dano.

WILL returns with notepad in hand. There's an uncomfortable pause.

WILL: (*Slapping DAN on the back.*) Hey, ladies, what's shakin'?

DAN: Not much.

WILL: Here's that press release...

MATT: (*Abruptly.*) Hey, guys, I'm pulling chocks. (*To WILL.*) Catch ya later, Wilbur.

WILL: Later, dude. (*Looking towards where MATT exited.*) On the rag?

DAN: Me?

WILL: Iron Man.

DAN: Oh, personal problems, I guess.

WILL: Probably Tammi... "the she-bitch from Selma." (*Pulling out a piece of paper and changing the subject.*) Tell me how this sounds.

DAN notices that WILL squints to read his own writing. WILL is unaware.

WILL: "Petty Officer JOE SCHMOE has just visited the... exotic city of Hong Kong where he sampled many authentic delicacies such as... Peking Duck and... Shark's Fin Soup."

DAN: How long have you been flying like this?

WILL: What's that?

DAN: Your eyes, Wilbur! Earlier you couldn't see when the lights went off in the stateroom now you're struggling to read your own handwriting...

WILL: It's just a minor eye infection. It's not affecting my flying.

DAN: Everything affects our flying. You should have the doc check your eyes.

WILL: No way... it might disqualify me for T.P.S. Eight hours sleep and I'll be fine.

DAN: We haven't had eight hours in the last eight years!

WILL: I'm fine, really. Would I lie to you? (He *raises three fingers in the Scouts salute.*) Promise. (*Slapping his shoulder with the notepad.*) Any ideas for this press release?

DAN: Sounds fine.

WILL: It sounds lame. P.A.O. wants it by twenty-hundred tonight.

DAN: (*Glancing at his watch.*) Impossible.

WILL: "Ours is not to question why."

DAN: I'm beginning to wonder about that.

WILL: Any pointers?

DAN: Stick to the facts. Short and sweet.

WILL: No way. The truth does not a good recruiting story make. (*Pause.*) Dinner in the Flag Mess?

DAN: How'd you know?

WILL: You can't be serious! "Ding Ding, Ding Ding, Commander in Chief Pacific Fleet Arriving"... six thousand men afraid to fart. It's like the second coming when your dad flies aboard. (*Pause.*) Iron Man eating with you and the Admiral?

DAN: He's a guest of the Chaplain. (*Changing the subject.*) Sometimes I try to imagine what it would be like if I didn't have my father always looking over my shoulder.

WILL: Yeah. I know what you mean.

DAN: No, not really. At least your dad gives you some breathing room. (*Turning to him.*) Remember how he used to kiss you whenever he came home from cruise? (*He reflects.*) I wonder why my father never did... and why your dad stopped?

WILL: Things changed after my mom died.

DAN: If I ever had a son I don't think I'd ever be able to stop kissing him.

WILL: "If"?

DAN: Yeah. I'm not sure I'll ever be ready to have children. I mean... how can a person help mold a child's life when he's still... in some ways... a kid himself?

WILL: You just do. You grow up together... it's "on the job training" all the way. I can't wait until Atticus and I will be able to throw a football together.

DAN: What if... what if he wants to play the piano... or sing... instead of playing ball?

WILL: No way. He won't.

DAN: But what if he does? What if he likes... singing Barry Manilow songs?

WILL: (*Rabbit punching him.*) I'll send him off to you. (*Changing the subject.*) So... did you and Matt have a good time the other night?

DAN: (*Awkwardly.*) Listen, I'm sorry about leaving you high and dry, buddy.

WILL: I was just curious about what you guys did.

DAN: Nothing much... just drank too much Tsing Tao beer. (*He looks up at the sky.*) Check it out. (*He snaps another picture.*)

WILL: (*Looking overhead.*) Wow.

DAN: I don't think I've ever seen it that blue before.

WILL throws his arm around DAN and recites a line from the poem "High Flight".

WILL: "Up, up the long, delirious burning blue..."

DAN joins him and they recite the next line in unison.

BOTH: "Where never Lark, or even Eagle flew..."

DAN stops. WILL continues reciting the poem.

WILL: "And while with silent lifting mind I've trod the high untrespassed sanctity of space... I put out my hand... and touched the face of God." *(Pause.)* Makes you believe anything's possible."

DAN: *(Looking up.)* Space.

WILL: *(Mimicking "Star Trek".)* The final frontier.

DAN: Someday.

WILL: Nothing's gonna stop us.

DAN turns and begins to confide in WILL.

DAN: Wilbur?

WILL: *(Still looking up.)* Yeah.

DAN: Did you ever have any... doubts... about... your attraction to Susan?

WILL: I knew it! You guys got laid last night... and now you're having second thoughts about Nancy.

DAN: No. I love Nance... it's just... I–

WILL: Look, you two have been dating for years maybe you both need some time apart.

DAN: *(Pause.)* Wilbur, It's not– Nancy's not the problem... there's something... there's someone–

WILL: I know. That little faggot civilian she's been seeing in Sausalito.

DAN: ... What?

WILL: *(Gently.)* Susan and I ran into them at Zack's a couple of months ago. I didn't wanna say anything in case– You've known about him for a while... right?

DAN: *(Shutting down.)* Yeah.

WILL: Listen, if the sex isn't happening... I mean– Suzie and I went through a dry patch right after Attie was born but... we were still into each other, or the idea of it at least.

DAN: *(Reflecting.)* She said they were just–

WILL: I wouldn't let her jerk you around too much longer.

DAN: She's not jerking me around...

WILL: I'm sorry. I didn't mean– Nance is great... but maybe it's not gonna work. (*He puts his arm around DAN.*) Whatever happens... my buddy always comes first. (*A beat. WILL looks at DAN.*) You okay?

DAN: Yeah. Thanks, Wilbur.

WILL: Hey, I'd better get crackin'. (*Referring to the press release.*) Would you proof this for me later?

DAN: Sure.

DAN begins to exit.

WILL: What do you say we meet for chow at nineteen hundred?

DAN: (*Lost in thought.*) What?

WILL: Unless you're already booked. You running with Matt again tonight?

DAN: No. No... dinner with my father in the Flag Mess, remember?

WILL: Oh, right. (*Tapping the notepad with his pencil.*) Just bullshit and hype, right Dano? Join the Navy and see the world... pass... you... by.

WILL moves stage left. Isolated, DAN looks out at the horizon. He exits after a beat.

Crossfade to

Scene 8

The Squadron Meeting Room. COKELY continues to interrogate WILL.

COKELY: So you discussed Hometown News Releases, photography and women? Nothing else?

WILL: That's it.

COKELY: Does your wife know you're interested in other women?

WILL: I didn't say– I'm not seeing *other* women!

COKELY: Oh? (*Walking around him and then leaning directly into WILL's face.*) Tell me, Will, how long have you and Lt. Lynch been having homosexual relations?

WILL: Excuse me? Is this–? You flew across the country because you think I'm– Special Agent Cokely, I am not a homosexual.

COKELY: Then how would you define your relationship with Lt. Lynch?

WILL: We've been best friends for years. (*Confused.*) Why?

COKELY: When one individual, a male, engages in sexual behavior with another individual, also male, we don't call them "friends" we call those men homosexuals. Now, perhaps you can...

WILL: I am very aware of the behavior that constitutes a homosexual act.

COKELY: And to what other officers in this squadron besides Lt. Lynch does this awareness extend?

WILL: I don't know where you came up with this idea. I'm very happily married.

COKELY: Really?

WILL: Yes. And I am straight. Heterosexual.

COKELY: You seemed awfully jumpy a few minutes ago, Will. (*Beat.*) Why would a normal man be worried if I talked to his father or Squadron Skipper about homosexuals?

WILL: I guess... guilt by association. What made you think I was–?

COKELY: Your buddy.

WILL: He told you *I* was gay!?

COKELY: Look Lieutenant, there's no need to get excited. The Washington office of the N.I.S. received a report a couple of weeks ago implicating your friend Lt. Lynch. He was seen engaged in a homosexual act during your last port call in Hong Kong.

WILL: I don't believe it! Where did you get your information?

COKELY: Lieutenant, your friend has already confessed. I'm just trying to save you and your father from being caught in the midst of a very unsavory situation.

WILL: I've got several things to do before my hop, Special Agent Cokely, this Q & A session is gonna have to wait. (*Quickly turning and walking away.*)

COKELY: I'm right behind you, Will.

WILL: (*Stopping abruptly.*) As one of the top ranking F-18 pilots in the fleet, I take exception to your accusations, I wanna know who's spreading this–

COKELY: Would you describe the other men in your squadron as outstanding Naval Officers and Aviators also?

WILL: I'd say so.

COKELY: Lt. Lynch?

WILL: Yes.

COKELY: Lt. Blackwood?

WILL: He was one of the best.

COKELY exits.
Blackout.

Scene 9

Three weeks earlier. MATT and CHARLIE, DAN and WILL are engaged in a game of Air Combat Maneuvers each flying in their separate planes. We hear the roar of jet engines. Individual specials light up each of their faces on an otherwise dark stage.

CHARLIE: I'm tellin' you, Iron Man, my dick was so hard a cat couldn't scratch it.

MATT: C'mon, Boner, Shore leave is over! Get your head out of Hong Kong and concentrate on flying your aircraft, you're about three minutes from jousting with Wilbur.

WILL: This is Wilbur, Eighty miles from mother I'm heading west two-seven-five. Got any tunes for us today, Iron Man?

MATT: That's a negative.

WILL: C'mon, Montovani, play us something.

CHARLIE: This lady was unbelievable, she had those green cat-shaped eyes that say "feed me and I'm yours"... and ohhh daawghy... a body built for speed!

MATT: Iron Man 120 miles from mother I'm headed east zero-niner-five.

CHARLIE: Jennifer. Jennifer Lord. Isn't that a beautiful name. (*No response.*) Iron Man?

The roar of the engines diminishes. A special illuminates MATT. He sees flashing colored lights and hears the pounding of disco music.

CHARLIE: Iron Man? Hey, partner you still with me?

MATT: (*The music and lights fade.*) What's your DME reading, Boner?

CHARLIE: Same as yours; I'm your wing-man remember?

MATT: Just tell me what your distance to mother is.

CHARLIE: One sixteen.

MATT: No joy. I don't see Will and Dano yet but we're closing on them fast.

CHARLIE: Pretty sure she was single too. Actually, she had that just-separated-but-not-yet-divorced look. She asked me which squadron I was attached to.

MATT: Just another WESTPAC Widow.

CHARLIE: Okay, call me a nugget, wet behind the ears... WESTPAC Widow?

MATT: How long have you been in the Navy? *Western Pacific.*

CHARLIE: I know it's an "easy woman" but why do we call 'em WESTPAC *Widows?*

DAN: Picture this Boner. It's 0900 and this lovely lady you're drooling over is kissing her husband goodbye... she stands on the pier and cries as his ship steams away to the Western Pacific for a six month cruise... she's a "widow" for six months. Now cut to the Officer's Club later that afternoon...

WILL: The time is 1700 sharp... "Happy Hour".

DAN: Guess who's propped up on a bar stool looking real appetizing waiting for you to buy her a drinkey pooh?

CHARLIE: Git out! Most of those ladies are really widowed...

DAN: That's a big negative, Boner.

WILL: Most of those women are *really* horny and most of our buddies are *really* snakes.

MATT: Hey, Dano, Wilbur, why don't you stay off our frequency till the games are over. Boner, keep your little head on the deck and your big head in the cockpit.

CHARLIE: Just seekin' some sage counsel.

MATT: Talley Ho! Bogey two o'clock high comin' at you, Boner, you take him I've got the bogey at one o'clock level.

DAN: One hundred miles from mother I'm heading west bearing two, seven, five. Talley Ho! Bogey ten o'clock low you take him, Wilbur, I've got one at eleven o'clock level.

WILL: (*Scanning the horizon.*) No joy. I don't see him.

DAN: (*Mimicking Mr.Ed the talking horse.*) C'mon Wilbur it's big as the nose on your face... one o'clock level now!

WILL: (*Scanning the entire horizon.*) No joy dammit! (*Suddenly.*) Belay my last! TalleyHo! Ten o'clock low about five miles!

DAN: HALLELLUYAH!

MATT: Fight's on!

CHARLIE: YEEHAW!

We hear the sound of jet engines as the four planes pass one another and the men jerk their heads to the rear, the side, up, and down following their prey.

CHARLIE: Smooth move, Wilbur. Hey, two can play this game. Hit the brakes! Here we go, I'm doublin' back and closin' in on your six.

WILL: Yeah, but can you catch me? Zone Five! I'm outta here. Dig my cheese, Boner!

DAN: C'mon Iron Man, show me what you've got.

The colored lights and disco music reappear for MATT. The specials dim on the other men.

DAN: C'mon, Iron Man, give me a fight. I didn't come out here for a turkey shoot. I'm closing in on you.

MATT: (*To himself.*) C'mon, dammit, focus. Focus! (*He sees DAN on his tail and makes an abrupt left upward movement.*) Catch me if you can! Selecting Zone Five afterburner.

DAN: (*DAN copies MATT's stick movements.*) I'm on your tail, big guy! Yeeeeeehaw!

MATT looks behind him and sees DAN again. He frantically jerks the stick hard right and turns to see DAN still on his tail.

DAN: History is about to be made! Sidewinder select!

MATT: (*Still Shaken.*) No... God Dammit... No!

DAN: What's wrong with you buddy? I'm closin' fast.

MATT: Jesus! I can't escape!

DAN: Fox Two.

MATT: (*Looking all around.*) Where the hell is he?

DAN: Check your six big guy. Tracking for guns.

MATT: Shit! (*Looking behind.*) Fight's off.

DAN: No way, you're mine!

MATT: I repeat Fight's off! I'm headed back to mother.

Lights out on MATT. He exits. After several beats WILL speaks.

WILL: Holy smokes... that's a first... "Captain Invincible" disengaged from a fight.

DAN: Let's take her in. Take my wing guys. Pigeons one zero five.

Crossfade to

Scene 10

Later. The Stateroom. Totally preoccupied, DAN wipes the sweat from his face as the other two men enter ribbing each other.

CHARLIE: Face it, Will, I was right on your six with my radar locked...

WILL: No way, Boner, you weren't on my tail! I rolled out before...

CHARLIE: (*Goosing him.*) Don't worry... I promise I won't tell a soul, they're not gonna take away your T.P.S. orders just cuz some nugget farm-boy flew circles around you.

WILL: Kiss my grits, Trumbo.

MATT enters towel-drying his hair, flight suit tied around his waist having just splashed his face and chest with water to cool off. Avoiding eye contact with the other guys he calmly places his towel in his locker and slings the synthesizer around his neck. Expressing an unconscious act of solidarity with MATT, DAN moves away from WILL and CHARLIE.

WILL: Hey, Liberace, what happened up there... lose your balls?

MATT suppresses his anger, places the headphones on his ears and begins to play. Aware of MATT's every movement, DAN is noticeably uncomfortable. He exits to the bathroom.

WILL: What mystery tune are you composing tonight, buddy?

No response. CHARLIE tries to spare MATT by distracting WILL.

CHARLIE: (*Showing WILL a picture in Penthouse.*) Hey, Wilbur, check these out!

WILL: Jesus. What do you do with those things?

CHARLIE: You need me to tell you...

WILL: Yeah, I've never used a milking machine before.

CHARLIE: "Bambi Marie McGillicutty... 38-24-36, five foot six, blonde hair"... everywhere? (*He turns the page.*) Yep!

"She loves sex on the beach... F-18 jocks with 12 inch cocks... and farm boys from Arkansas"!

WILL: In your dreams...

Suddenly another power surge and the lights flicker off and on again.

CHARLIE: What the...?!

MATT: A billion dollar toy with no instruction manual! (*Looking up at the ceiling.*) Read the fuckin' directions assholes!

WILL: Two attempts to land aboard the carrier? I don't know, maybe he should think about a career in music.

CHARLIE: (*Trying to distract him.*) You ever consider doin' somethin' else, Wilbur?

WILL: What is this, Boner, twenty questions?

CHARLIE: Just curious. I mean, you guys have wanted to be jet jocks and astronauts your entire lives. Didn't you ever wonder what it was like in the real world?

WILL: We know. Just a bunch of pig farmers with sons who have twelve-inch cocks.

DAN enters in his flight suit having just washed his face.

CHARLIE: Serious now, Dano, is it cause your daddy flew?

DAN: What's that?

WILL: We do this to protect and preserve the American Way.

CHARLIE: (*Making a game-show buzzer sound.*) AAGH! Try again.

MATT takes off his headphones but doesn't turn around. He fiddles with his guitar.

WILL: (*Remembering.*) My grandpa had a thousand acres of wheat and corn in central Nebraska. Every August, regardless of how far away we were stationed, my parents would ship me out there and I'd help with the harvest.

CHARLIE: You're kiddin'...

DAN: Nope, my folks sent me out there too.

WILL: (*Continuing.*) There was this enormous empty silo that my Grandpa used as a hangar for his old yellow Stearman Biplane... it was perfect except part of its upper wing was missing. Dano and I used to spend hours in that dusty old cockpit pretending we were flying... shouting and laughing... imagining the wind in our face.

DAN: I think that was when I first realized that I wanted to fly.

WILL: (*Putting his arm around DAN.*) More than anything, I wanted to be up in that plane looking down on those fields... following the roads from farm to farm... seeing how they were connected to one another from above.

CHARLIE: Did you and your Grandaddy ever get 'er flyin'?

WILL: We planned to fix the wing the summer before we entered the Academy but... he died that spring... the farm was sold and that was that. (*In reverie.*) Someday I'm gonna have so much altitude I'll be able to see the continents and the oceans wrapped around the earth... be able to watch all the planets in the solar system revolve around the sun.

CHARLIE: Still waters run deep.

WILL: (*He snaps out of his reverie.*) What about you, why are you doing this, Boner?

CHARLIE: Because its the funnest damn thing I've ever done... with my pants on! I'm a speed junkie! Just say YES to 1200 knots and 9 G's of thrust!

WILL: (*They high five.*) Halleluyah!

CHARLIE: (*Remembering.*) There was one flight I'll never forget.

DAN: Why's that?

CHARLIE: I jerked off up there. It was down in Pensacola... I was flyin' over the beach and out into the gulf preparing to rendezvous with the carrier... and I remember thinkin' "the only thing that could make this more perfect would

be makin' love up here with the woman of my
dreams." Try as I might, I just couldn't keep a lid on
my imagination. So as I accelerated into the groove on
my final approach... when I knew I was right on glide
path... I pulled my puppy out and spanked him all the
way down. (*They're all laughing.*) Landin' on the deck of
that carrier was like drivin' a '63 stingray 150 miles an
hour smack into a brick wall with Bambie Marie's lips
wrapped around my pecker!

WILL: You're like a juke-box full of country music.

CHARLIE: How's that?

WILL: Frighteningly honest.

DAN: You want to hear frightening? (*To CHARLIE.*) Tell him
what you told me the other day... about the pig.

CHARLIE: The Pig?... Oh, Yeah! My cousin, Larry, lived
in Colorado so we didn't see that much of one another
growin' up but when he did visit... well, we used to have
this six-hundred pound sow named Debbie... and we'd
take turns holding her while the other one hid the sausage.

WILL: Impossible...

CHARLIE: One time– in fact it was the last summer Larry
ever visited– I was goin' to town on Debbie while Larry
held her still in the corner of this pen in the barn and all
of a sudden his face went all long and white as a ghost.
So I turned behind me to see what he was lookin' at...
and there was my mama... in her hair curlers and her
old pink bathrobe holdin' a drinkin' glass full of gin...
just starin' at us. (*To MATT who can't suppress his laughter.*)
I'm not sure who passed out first... but we all went down...
we all went down in the end.

WILL: Boner, you're stranger than fiction.

CHARLIE: You should meet my cousin, Larry.

*CHARLIE playfully grabs WILL, puts him in a headlock and
twists his ear.*

*While CHARLIE and WILL are occupied DAN attempts to
engage MATT.*

DAN: Listen, I'm sorry if I pushed you too hard up there today, I...

MATT: Forget it.

DAN: Maybe I shouldn't have engaged as early–

MATT: (*Standing and throwing his headphones down.*) Give it a rest! I fucked up, okay!? Period. (*He goes to his locker, slams it shut and turns before exiting.*) The taxpayers get nervous if they hear the warriors sniveling.

> *They're all startled by MATT's outburst. After MATT exits, WILL looks over at CHARLIE and then DAN for an explanation. They both look away.*
>
> *CHARLIE exits as COKELY enters with WILL's flight helmet.*
>
> *Crossfade to*

Scene 11

> *The present. The Squadron Hangar COKELY continues to question WILL.*

COKELY: So all three of you were headed for Test Pilot School after this upcoming cruise?

WILL: That's right.

COKELY: Being selected for T.P.S... that's a pretty impressive achievement, Lieutenant, wouldn't you agree?

WILL: Guess so.

COKELY: Only the top– what– one percent of all Naval Aviators would even be considered, right?

WILL: I'm not sure of the exact percentage.

COKELY: A guy on the road to becoming an astronaut would have to be pretty perceptive... clued into the people around him... attention to detail and all that.

WILL: That's correct.

COKELY: You didn't have any suspicions about Lt. Lynch's–?

WILL: No! Agent Cokely, I'm running late, I need–

COKELY: I presume you've undressed in his presence?

WILL: Yes.

COKELY: Showered, slept?

WILL: Yes.

COKELY: You spent a night alone together in the woods near Mobile Bay after punching out of a TA-4.

WILL: That was five years ago... we were in a survival situation. Listen, I've got–

COKELY: And nothing in his behavior led you to believe–

WILL: No! Never! I didn't know anything about this until yesterday when he told me about going to some night club in Hong Kong with Lt. Black– (*He stops.*)

COKELY: ... Blackwood? Thank you. (*He leans in for emphasis.*) So... your best friends were schtuppin' each other right under your nose. How does that make you feel?

WILL: What do you mean?

COKELY: Lynch and Blackwood had a secret life that didn't include you. (*WILL considers this. He looks anguished.*) When do you suppose they first had anal intercourse?

WILL: I have to prepare for a flight. (*He begins to walk away.*)

COKELY: (*Handing a photograph to WILL.*) Can you identify the people in this photo?

WILL: (*Looking at it closely.*) I'm pretty sure that's... me, Lt. Lynch, Charlie and Matt Blackwood in Italy last year.

COKELY: Pretty sure? Lieutenant, that is *you* on the left?

WILL: Yes. But it's not what you think it is...

COKELY: It isn't? I see four naked or partially clad Naval officers lying around a hilltop goosing one another.

WILL: Look, you've got the wrong idea. We had three days of leave in Italy, we'd been to the Vatican, the Sistine, the day before... we were recreating one of the murals painted on the ceiling... we were all trashed... it was just a spoof, an innocent fraternity stunt.

COKELY: Whose idea was it?

WILL: It was just... one of those spontaneous things.

COKELY: Well, Lieutenant, this spontaneous thing could cost you quite a lot. You do realize as one of the "top ranking" F-18 pilots in the United States Navy you're subject to certain expectations regarding your conduct?

WILL: Yes.

COKELY: What kind of an officer parades around the Italian countryside in the raw?

WILL: We were on leave. There was nobody around for miles.

COKELY: Was it Lynch's idea to take the photograph?

WILL: (*After a long hesitation.*) I suppose so.

COKELY: And which one of you initiated the gay sex orgy afterward?

WILL: There was no–! Listen– how much more of this do I have to...?

COKELY: I have a couple more routine questions.

WILL: (*Checking his watch.*) I'm five minutes away from a preflight brief...

COKELY: Have you ever had sex with a person of the same gender.

WILL: No.

COKELY: A parent?

WILL: Do you mean my own parents or someone that is a parent. My wife is a parent, I have sex with her... is that okay?

COKELY: A child of either gender under the age of twelve?

WILL: No, I have not.

COKELY: Have you ever engaged in, desired to engage in or do you intend to engage in sex with people of other nationalities, members of the communist party... or small animals?

WILL: No. No. And... no. These are routine questions?

WILL exits. COKELY walks into following scene.

Crossfade to

Scene 12

The present. Later that morning. The Stateroom. COKELY is searching through the lockers. He stops, picks up an officer's cap and touches the insignia on it reverentially. He places it on his head and admires himself in the mirror. CHARLIE enters in his Dress Blues.

CHARLIE: Can I help you?

COKELY: (*Quickly removing the hat.*) Lt. Trumbo! (*Extending his hand.*) Special Agent John Cokely, N.I.S. When was the last time you spoke with Lt. Lynch?

CHARLIE: Yesterday at the Airport in Arlington... after the burial. Why, is he okay?

COKELY: He's being held in Washington for questioning.

CHARLIE: Questioning?

COKELY: (*Picking up a photograph of DAN's girlfriend, Nancy.*) This your gal?

CHARLIE: No. That's Nancy, Dan's girlfriend. How is he?

COKELY: Fine. (*Still holding the picture and looking around the room.*) She live in the city too?

CHARLIE begins to undress.

CHARLIE: Yes, sir. What's up with–?

COKELY: Where's your gal?

CHARLIE: I don't have one.

COKELY: You like girls, don't you?

CHARLIE: Girls? I liked *girls* when I was a kid. (*Pause.*) I like *women* now.

COKELY: (*Picks up a picture of Susan Stephensen.*) Will Stephensen's wife, right?

CHARLIE: Yeah, a real angel. How'd you know?

COKELY: N.I.S., remember? (*CHARLIE nods.*) So, why don't you have any pictures of these *women* you fancy?

CHARLIE: I do.

COKELY: Can I see them?

CHARLIE: No. (*He waits a beat and then points to his head.*)

They're all up here. (*Beat.*) You mind if I take a shower? I'm kinda stinky, just got off a long flight.

COKELY: (*Looking at picture of Nancy again.*) Lynch and his girl– they live together?

CHARLIE: They did for awhile.

COKELY: What happened?

CHARLIE: Life.

COKELY: Life?

CHARLIE: (*Miming his hand soaking in Palmolive Dish Detergent.*) You're soakin' in it.

COKELY: Yeah. When they hit their late twenties they turn into rabbits. She probably needed someone with endurance... someone that can go all night long.

CHARLIE: Even rabbits need a soft touch. I'll put my money on tenderness over endurance any day of the week. So, what is it you came to talk about, Special Agent Cokely?

COKELY: You've been in the same squadron with Lt. Lynch for the past...?

CHARLIE: Eleven months. Why?

COKELY: You share the same stateroom with him. You shoot the shit with each other?

CHARLIE: Yes.

COKELY: Has he said anything... have you noticed any strange behavior from him in the time you've been bunking together?

Refusing to become intimidated, CHARLIE stares directly at COKELY but remains silent.

COKELY: Lt. Trumbo?

CHARLIE: No, sir.

COKELY: I understand Will Stephensen and his wife had friends over to their quarters last Sunday evening. Was Lt. Lynch there?

CHARLIE: Yes, Sir. It was a lovely welcome home get-together.

COKELY: Was Lt. Lynch's girlfriend there?

CHARLIE: No.

COKELY: He and Nancy still doing the dirty deed?

CHARLIE: *Dirty?*

COKELY: Yeah. Is he fucking the little lady?

CHARLIE: *Fucking?*

COKELY: Why wasn't she at the welcome home party last week?

CHARLIE: I couldn't rightly say...

COKELY: But they still see one another?

CHARLIE: Well she was waitin' for him on the pier when the ship pulled in last week. Lookin' mighty pretty, I might add.

Crossfade to

Scene 13

Two months earlier. DAN's apartment in San Francisco. He stands downstage in his boxer shorts, looking out the window. Nancy enters, presumably from the bedroom, wearing a robe. Music plays very softly. (Pat Metheny's "Tell Her You Saw Me")

NANCY: It's nice being here. I've missed you. (*Pause.*) What is it, Danny?

DAN: A crystal clear night in San Francisco... the moon shining on the bay.

NANCY: That's heavenly. Exhilarating.

DAN: You deserve heavenly.

NANCY: (*Pause.*) So do you.

She kisses him. After a few moments he pulls away. She turns and goes to the chair.

NANCY: Earlier this evening I sensed... I guess we can't keep ignoring this.

DAN: He treats you well?

A beat. She finally nods.

DAN: "How's the sex" he boldly asks, finally acknowledging the dead dog they've been stepping over for the past...

NANCY: Danny, do we have to...

DAN: Yes. We're both professionals when it comes to avoiding the issues.

NANCY: That's true. You get it honest.

DAN: I do?

NANCY: (*Laughing nervously.*) Your mother. The original Pollyanna. Every time I see some road kill I think of her.

DAN: (*He laughs.*) To this day she still says the same thing every time.

NANCY: You can't be serious.

DAN: Dead serious. "Look at that poor little opossum sleeping by the side of the road."

NANCY: She must know they've been run over...

DAN: No. The last time I tried to tell her they were dead we were living in London so I must have been about... ten...

NANCY: And she threatened to wash your mouth out with soap?

DAN: No. Cold Cream.

NANCY: Oh, my God... that's right. Only *your* mother would wash out her children's mouths with Cold Cream. What *class*.

DAN: What an idiotic punishment.

NANCY: I never really thought about it until now.

He moves away.

DAN: So I guess it must be good?

She recoils.

NANCY: Please, Danny...

He presses her.

DAN: Is it?

NANCY: Do we really need to...?

DAN: Does he use the "I" word?

NANCY: As in "I" love you?

DAN: He's in love with you?

NANCY: I think so.

55

DAN: And you? Are you in love with him?

He turns to her. She shakes her head. Her love for DAN is evident.

DAN: Does he turn you on?

NANCY: Please...

DAN: Does he?

An excruciating pause. She nods.

DAN: What's it like... being completely turned on by each other? Exhilarating?

On the verge of shattering. She nods.

NANCY: I've prayed for it.

DAN: Me too.

She goes to him and kisses him passionately. He responds... but after several beats it's evident his body and his heart aren't in sync. We see his pain as he pulls away again. After a few moments he collects himself and begins putting on his clothes.

DAN: You sure you're not gonna come to the party?

NANCY: (*She begins to break.*) Let's give it some time. I can be satisfied with nice.

DAN: No you can't.

NANCY: Yes... I can.

DAN: Content maybe... truly happy and satisfied, I bet not.

NANCY: I'll probably grow tired of exhilaration.

DAN: No. Exhilaration will evolve into nice. If you start out with nice you'll end up numb and bored.

NANCY: But what about you, Danny? What do you want?

DAN: (*Looking out.*) The fog's rollin' in again. I hope it doesn't cover the moon.

Crossfade.

We begin to hear disco music as the lights dim on DAN. As NANCY turns away from him she ends up standing in a pool of deep red light. NANCY exits and MATT enters the pool of red light dancing to the erotic pounding of the music. DAN turns and joins him.

Crossfade to

Scene 14

That night. WILL and SUSAN are hosting a party at their quarters. DAN and MATT dance together. A disco beat (Primal Scream: Screamadelica) and colored lights make it clear they have momentarily forgotten themselves and are transported back to the night in Hong Kong. The disco music becomes Barry White's "You're the First, My Last, My Everything". WILL dances with SUSAN as CHARLIE looks on.

CHARLIE: Come on, Wilbur, you're only experiencin' half of everything in life if your hips are locked. (*To SUSAN.*) That's it! That's where it all comes from. Where life begins.

CHARLIE: Look at Dano and Mattie. Sell it, Iron Man!

DAN and MATT are brought back to reality by CHARLIE's comment. They separate abruptly. MATT grabs SUSAN and begins dancing with her.

CHARLIE: (*To WILL.*) Ever wonder why people smile a lot after they've been makin' love? It's a physical thing. (*He demonstrates.*) Ya see the hip bone's connected directly to the Smile Zone.

DAN: I think you're onto something, Boner.

SUSAN: (*Looking around.*) Where's Tammi?

CHARLIE: Outside talking with the Chaplain.

WILL changes the tape and puts on another old tune. (Vikki Carr's "Can't Take My Eyes Off of You") Within seconds DAN and MATT are arm-in-arm doing the can-can. Feeling ignored, WILL jumps in between them. MATT pulls CHARLIE up into the line.

TAMMI: (*Entering and turning down the music.*) The Chaplain's such a kind and thoughtful man, if I didn't know better I'd swear he was a Baptist.

MEN: (*Still doing the Can-Can.*) I LOVE THE CHAPLAIN! DA DA DA DADA DA!

TAMMI: (*Having marched over to where SUSAN is putting birthday cake on plates.*) A case of beer's been drunk already?!

MEN: (*Still dancing.*) We're drunk already! DA DA DA DADA DA!

TAMMI: What about the baby?

WILL: Oh, he's fine, Charlie taught him how to jerk off so he'll sleep through the night.

MEN: (*Singing in a stage whisper.*) What about the baby!

TAMMI: Fooey!

> *She marches over to the stereo and turns it off. Everyone stops dancing and looks at TAMMI... MATT and DAN realize they're arm-in-arm and separate abruptly. Searching for something to alleviate the awkwardness of the moment, DAN gets his camera.*

DAN: Okay everyone... photo op! (*Everyone awkwardly acquiesces.*)

CHARLIE: (*Recovering.*) A toast! To Wilbur... Happy birthday!

> *Everyone raises their glass or bottle in tribute.*

SUSAN: (*Raising her bottle and addressing them.*) To our friendship, may it never wane!

MATT: To Susan, soon to be the best new Massage Therapist at the Naval Hospital. (*To WILL.*) You should be proud, Wilbur.

WILL: (*Kissing SUSAN.*) I am... very.

> *They all raise their bottles again.*

DAN: (*DAN takes a candid photo and then raises his bottle.*) "To Atticus William Stephensen the First."

CHARLIE: The "one and only"...

MATT: Like his namesakes may he be an inspiration to us all!

WILL: Here! Here! (*They all tap bottles.*) Thanks, guys.

TAMMI: (*Raising her Pepsi.*) To... world peace!

SUSAN: What a... wonderful thought. Here! Here!

WILL: Wonderfully unrealistic. (*He gets a piece of cake.*)

CHARLIE: Funny you should say that, Tam, while I was waitin' for the pizza I noticed this poster on the wall, it was a picture of the earth all green and blue and the words below it said "Visualize World Peace."

WILL: Was there one next to it that said "Nuke the Whales"?

CHARLIE: I've been repeatin' those words over and over in my head for the past hour.

WILL: Well don't start visualizing it too, or we'll all be out of a job. (*They laugh.*)

SUSAN: (*Passing out cake to everyone.*) Maybe we are on the road to world peace. The Berlin Wall is coming down. I know this may be crazy but wouldn't it be great if we could just shut everything down?

TAMMI: Yeah! We could turn the bases into solar energy fields... convert all the F-18's to two-seaters and use 'em for joyrides.

SUSAN: (*Looking at WILL.*) Just think how wonderful it would be knowing that each day instead of preparing for war you were going to take people up in an F-18 and give them the thrill of a lifetime!

WILL: That's irrational thinking, honey. Anyway, the USSR is not going to abandon communism.

SUSAN: Never say never. A few years ago nobody knew how to talk to an answering machine... now you can't get 'em to shut up. (*Getting up.*) I'm just happy to have you all home safe and sound for a couple of weeks.

TAMMI: I'll second that! Did you know that a total of nine people have died aboard the Truman in the past 18 months? It was in the Chronicle this morning. Isn't that frightening! (*She sits on MATT's lap.*) That's why I want my Matthew out of the Navy.

WILL: The population of a Super Carrier is greater than most small cities in this country. That's about par for the course, Tammi.

DAN: It's a dangerous world in or out of the military.

CHARLIE: This cake is deeelicious! You get it, Dano? (*DAN shakes his head no.*)

SUSAN: (*To WILL.*) It came from that great little bakery in The Castro.

TAMMI: The Castro? Isn't that the gay district?

SUSAN: Yeah. That's where we got the cake yesterday, remember?

TAMMI: No, this came from that bakery in that row of pretty little Victorian shops.

SUSAN: That was it.

TAMMI: No, no these were too well kept and clean... almost military like... everything in its proper place.

SUSAN: That *was* The Castro, Tammi. Ya know, it wouldn't be such a bad place for you to sell your Karrie Mae beauty products.

MATT steals a glance at DAN. They appear uncomfortable.

CHARLIE: Susan has a point there, Tam, Karrie Mae makes stuff for men, right? You should go door to door. You'd be rich before nightfall.

TAMMI: But I'd be scared to go down there alone.

WILL: They'd probably be scared of you.

TAMMI: Why, Will? I'm the normal one. Even the bible says they should be punished.

CHARLIE: You know, Tam, in all the churches I've been in, I've yet to see a stained glass window depictin' Jesus wieldin' a baseball bat.

MATT: He had bigger fish to fry, so to speak.

TAMMI: (*Turning on MATT.*) I'm not for gay bashin'!
I just think it's sad that they'll never really be accepted. Like the children of an interracial marriage... the parents may be able to handle it but the kids are caught in the middle not knowing where they belong.
I think most of the gay people don't really want to be outcasts, which they are, I think deep down inside they wish they could have regular lives with children and grandchildren and not have to worry about all of their friends gettin' beat up and gettin' AIDS.

Everyone is silent for a moment.

SUSAN: (*To TAMMI.*) Well... I'm sure there's nothing to be afraid of.

WILL: (*Turning to DAN.*) Hey! How do you fit four queers on a bar stool?

DAN looks cornered.

SUSAN: Please, let's not start with the same old jokes again.

WILL: Anyone?

CHARLIE: (*Sullenly.*) You turn it over.

TAMMI: (*Pause.*) I'm not gettin' it.

WILL: Obviously.

DAN: (*To MATT.*) I think I'm gonna head home. What do you say we do a ten-miler tomorrow?

TAMMI: (*To MATT.*) Did you see that new BMW in the driveway?

WILL: (*Looks at SUSAN.*) It's not new, it's my Dad's.

DAN: (*To MATT who is ignoring him.*) What do you say, Matt?

SUSAN: Will's dad hasn't been able to drive since he's been sick so he had it shipped across country. I haven't used it once.

DAN: Matt?

MATT: Yeah– whatever– I don't know now. I'll call you.

TAMMI: (*To MATT.*) A new BMW and they haven't even driven it? (*To WILL.*) When did it arrive?

DAN: (*To MATT.*) Hey, I thought you said we were gonna run–

MATT: (*Blowing up.*) I don't know, Dan! (*To TAMMI.*) I told you all this today, Tammi!!

There's a deafening silence. In an effort to diffuse the tension CHARLIE goes to the stereo.

CHARLIE: Hey... let's get this party crankin'. This is that album I wanted you to...

TAMMI: (*To MATT.*) All you ever want to do is play your cotton-pickin guitar and run with Dan! You promised we could go shoppin' for a new car tomorrow! (*She storms out.*)

SUSAN: (*After an awkward silence.*) What's she so upset about?

WILL: Maybe she's feeling left-out.

MATT: (*Standing.*) I'd better go home with my wife. (*He kisses SUSAN.*) Thanks.

He exits.

WILL: There's some heavy ju-ju in the air tonight. What's up with him, Dano?

DAN: (*Guiltily.*) How would I know?

WILL: That's harder than Chinese arithmetic.

DAN: What?

WILL: Trying to figure out how in the hell he married that cunt.

SUSAN: Will! You know how I hate that word! She's not that bad.

WILL: Neither was Pol Pot.

SUSAN: (*To DAN.*) Are you okay, Dano?

DAN: Yeah.

CHARLIE: (*He knows what's up.*) Hey, I've gotta run... late date... sweet young thing. (*He kisses SUSAN and hugs WILL.*) I had an outstandin' time.

SUSAN: The pizza was delicious, honey... we'll talk tomorrow?

CHARLIE: Absolutely. (*He kisses her again and gives DAN a bear hug.*) See ya, studly.

CHARLIE exits.

SUSAN: Dano, can I get you something to drink?

DAN: No. Thanks. I've had enough.

WILL: C'mon, don't be such a lightweight.

SUSAN: (*Pause.*) Are you sure everything's okay?

DAN: (*Smiling too brightly.*) Everything's fine.

WILL: (*To SUSAN.*) I'll take another.

SUSAN exits. There is an uncomfortable silence.

WILL: Why don't you wanna have another brew with your buddy?

DAN: Because I'm...

WILL: Because I can't run consecutive sixes like Iron Man?
I'm not a challenge for you anymore?

DAN: Wilbur– You've got a zero-six-hundred eye exam in
the morning... remember?

SUSAN returns empty handed.

SUSAN: No cold ones, honey.

WILL: Okay... how about some single malt? Dano? One
shot?

DAN acquiesces to WILL and nods.

WILL: Susan, do you mind?

SUSAN: (*Putting her arms around him from behind.*) Honey–
Dan is taking a day of leave to watch Atticus so we can
get away tomorrow and you've got your annual physical.
Please... I really don't want you comatose in the
morning. (*Brightly.*) Coffee? With a scoop of Haagen
Dasz? How 'bout it men?

WILL: (*Removing her arms from around him.*) I'd like to
relax and spend some time with my buddy. I'll be
in later.

SUSAN: (*Taken aback.*) Oh... okay.

DAN: (*Getting up.*) Hey, guys, it was a great evening.
I– I'm gonna call it a night... I'll see you tomorrow.
Happy birthday, Wilbur.

*He kisses SUSAN, punches WILL's arm and exits. There's an
awkward silence. SUSAN begins cleaning up the room.*

SUSAN: What's eating you, honey? (*No response. She
continues picking up for several beats.*) Listen, I know you're
worried about your dad, Will, but– I don't know why
you insisted on telling that stupid fag joke. (*No response.*)
Do you really think Dano's okay? (*No response.*) Well...
do you know what's up with Mattie?

WILL: He's married to Cruella deVille.

SUSAN: Come on, talk to me, honey.

WILL: Isn't that what I'm doing?

SUSAN: (*She tries to put her arms around him.*) You know what I mean.

WILL: No! I don't know what you mean! I'm turning in. (*He exits into the bedroom.*)

Completely stunned, SUSAN stands all alone in the room.

SUSAN: Happy birthday!

Slow fade to black.

End of Act One.

ACT TWO

Scene 1

The present. The Stateroom aboard ship. We hear the sound of running water and hear CHARLIE singing offstage. Perturbed, COKELY stands holding a towel and shampoo.

COKELY: Lieutenant?

CHARLIE: Pardon me, Special Agent Cokely, would you kindly repeat the last question? (*Sticking his head out of the shower.*) Time to "de-Valdez" my hair. Could you toss me my shampoo?

COKELY tosses it to him and CHARLIE pretends to fumble it. He looks at COKELY with a smile.

CHARLIE: Oops... almost dropped it. (*He steps back into the shower.*)

COKELY: Lieutenant Trumbo... am I interfering with your routine!?

CHARLIE: Not at all, I have a lunch date in the city... wanna be fresh as a daisy.

COKELY: Well, it looks like you might have to cancel those plans.

CHARLIE: Nah, I'm pretty good at pattin' my head and rubbin' my belly at the same time.

COKELY: I don't have all day, Lieutenant.

CHARLIE: That makes two of us. See, I knew we had somethin' in common.

CHARLIE steps out of the shower naked. COKELY looks away completely flustered.

CHARLIE: What's wrong? Never seen a grown man without his clothes on?

COKELY: (*Throwing the towel at him.*) Did you notice any unusual behavior from Lieutenants Lynch or Blackwood after your last port call?

CHARLIE: Like I told you, I don't think so.

CHARLIE finishes drying off and puts on his shorts.

COKELY: What were you and your buddies doing in a gay club in Hong Kong?

CHARLIE: Gay club? Who saw me at a gay club?

COKELY: Don't fuck with me, Lieutenant! Lynch has already admitted to it. Did you see Will Stephensen with him?

CHARLIE: Now just hold your horses there, Mr. Special Agent Man. Why don't you ask Lt. Stephensen? I'm sure he can answer that question better than me. Did you ask him?

COKELY: Yes.

CHARLIE: And what was his response?

COKELY: He said he wasn't there.

CHARLIE: Next question.

COKELY: Was Lt. Blackwood there?

CHARLIE: You sure don't learn very fast.

COKELY: Okay, where were *you* the night of August 13th?

CHARLIE: I spent most of the evening at the Peninsula Hotel with two aviators from the other Hornet squadron. We were entertaining a couple of ladies on leave from Yokosuka (YO-KU-SKAH). After I left them I went to a night club called "Disco-Disco" for a grand total of about ten minutes...

COKELY: "Disco-Disco"? You do realize you were in a homosexual establishment?

CHARLIE: No! Well I'll be damned! Come to think of it I do remember seein' a lot of men dancin' with men. Were those homosexuals?

COKELY: (*Showing CHARLIE a photo.*) Why don't you tell me about this photograph.

CHARLIE: Taken last year... we were on leave in Italy. (*Taking photo.*) This is embarrassing...

COKELY: That's understandable...

CHARLIE: Because, I promise you, this photo makes my johnson look about half it's actual size. (*Grinning at COKELY.*) Wouldn't you agree?

COKELY: Lieutenant, I'm sure the N.I.S. couldn't care less about the size of your...

CHARLIE: (*Snapping.*) Oh, is that so?! Well, it seems to me all you've been doing for the last thirty minutes is asking questions about where my shipmates did or didn't go dancin' with or without other men in some gay or straight night-club. Well why don't we just torch that bush you've been beatin' around and cut to the chase. You wanna' know what makes their peckers hard? I don't know and I don't give a rat's ass as long as they can cut the Gray Poupon when the shit hits the fan. They can go hump a tree if that revs their engine. Even if I did know, it's not my place to share their personal lives with you. Now in reference to me, not that it's any business of yours or the Joint Chiefs, I like putting my pecker in a pretty pink... vagina. How's that for alliteration?

COKELY: I'm not interested in your English skills, Lieutenant. But you're good. Very good. Thank you for your information. (*Looks at his watch.*) Luckily for you, I have another appointment I need to prepare for.

CHARLIE: My life has always been punctuated with a seemingly inordinate amount of luck.

COKELY: You may need it. Now before we end this *initial* session, I have a few routine questions.

CHARLIE: I'm good with routines. Fire away.

COKELY: Is Lt. Lynch a homosexual?

CHARLIE: He never copped my knob.

COKELY: Are you a homosexual?

CHARLIE: No.

COKELY: Have you ever engaged in, desired to engage in or do you intend to engage in sex with people of other nationalities, members of the Communist party or small animals?

CHARLIE: (*Pause.*) Define small.

Blackout.

Scene 2

The present. A light comes up on SUSAN talking on the telephone stage left. Stage right another light comes up on TAMMI also on the telephone. She's wearing a bathrobe.

TAMMI: I was hopin' my friends would be there to meet me... but I haven't heard anything. At least my mamma will be waitin' at the airport when I land. How's Will's daddy doin'?

SUSAN: Oh, he's fine, Tam, back at the Pentagon working hard against all advice... we're worried about you.

TAMMI: I'm a survivor. I just need to get away from all of this for a couple of weeks before I can even think about packin' up the rest of my things.

SUSAN: You must be exhausted, Will and I would love to take you to dinner and...

TAMMI: I'm not feelin' very sociable. Can I take a rain check?

A doorbell rings in SUSAN's home distracting her.

SUSAN: Of course. (*To door.*) Come in! (*To TAMMI.*) Remember, if you get lonely tonight we're just down the street. You're always welcome.

TAMMI: I've got the first flight out so I'm goin' to bed early. Susan?

SUSAN: Yes?

TAMMI: If you speak to Dan... tell him I'm praying for him.

SUSAN: I will. Promise you'll take care and call us when you get back from Selma?

TAMMI: Cross my heart. Bye bye.

Lights out on TAMMI. SUSAN hangs up and turns towards the door as Agent COKELY enters.

COKELY: Excuse me, are you Lt. Stephensen's wife?

SUSAN: Oh, my God. (*Almost faint.*) What's happened to Will?

COKELY: Nothing. You're husband's fine. I'm John Cokely, Naval Investigative Service. I need to ask you some questions.

We hear a baby begin to cry.

SUSAN: Excuse me, please.

Crossfade to

The present. The Interrogation Room at the Pentagon. DAN's Jacket is off and his head is on the desk. Jones, holding a folded newspaper is staring at the ceiling. DAN lifts his head.

DAN: Can't we call it a day?

JONES: I don't have the authority to terminate this meeting.

DAN: Meeting? I told you everything I know hours ago. (*He looks at his watch.*) Almost twenty hours ago. I really need to get back to my...

The telephone rings.

JONES: (*Answering the phone.*) Yeah. (*To DAN.*) Lieutenant, why don't you take five... don't go any further than the soda machine at the end of the hall. (*DAN exits.*)

Crossfade to

SUSAN and WILL's quarters. COKELY is alone on the telephone.

JONES: What a surprise, I thought you'd been run over by a Trolley Car.

COKELY: Listen, I can't talk now, I'm at Stephensen's quarters...

JONES: Where's my sandwich?

COKELY: Fuck you, Jonesie. Is he talking?

JONES: No. And I don't think he's...

COKELY: Lynch is definitely guilty. His buddy ratted on him. I also found some interesting photos in the Stateroom. I've hit the mother lode out here in sunny California. Listen, I need a written statement. I want names of every military and civilian guy he's ever been with or we inform his old man, the Admiral, about this inquiry.

JONES: I thought you were trying to bury this? Come on, John...

COKELY: You don't bury something till it's dead.

JONES: Any more leads on the informant?

COKELY: No. I was hoping you'd made some headway.

JONES: Like I said... he's not talking.

COKELY: What if he thought his squadron buddies or his girlfriend were gonna find out?

JONES: They probably already know.

COKELY: No way. You think he'd have this many friends if they knew he was queer?

JONES: Come on back, John, I'm tired of playing bad cop.

COKELY: I don't like it anymore than you do, but we're gonna have to be firm with him to help him... so don't let him sleep. The less he naps the more he yaps.
I want names.

Crossfade to

Pentagon Interrogation Room. DAN has returned with a soda for Jones too.

JONES: (*Taking soda and opening it.*) Tell me something, Lieutenant. Have you accepted that you're different?

DAN: I don't understand.

JONES: Oh, I think you do, Dan. Seems your buddies out in Alameda have been spillin' the beans. (*A beat.*) You want everyone to like you, don't you?

DAN: Sir?

JONES: I didn't ask for a soda.

DAN: I simply thought...

JONES: No such thing as a simple thought. There's no need for you to look after me... we're not on your side. But you chose to overlook that... which tells me there's a demon in your gut that secretly talks to your head every moment of every day and it says "I'm different... I better work extra hard to cover it up". (*He pauses.*)

Sooner or later a man's gotta stand up and be counted. Whatever the cost. I was just paintin' by numbers until I accepted that this (*Touching his face.*) is part of who I am. It won't wash off.

Crossfade to

SUSAN's quarters. SUSAN enters. She and COKELY begin talking.

SUSAN: I apologize for the interruption. He usually doesn't cry like that.

COKELY: I'm sorry if I scared you. Would you mind if I asked you a few questions?

SUSAN: Not at all. Please, have a seat.

COKELY: The Truman returned a week ago Friday, correct?

SUSAN: A week ago Saturday. My husband and I had a party here the following evening.

COKELY: Right... I've heard you're quite a hostess. Now, I don't enjoy this, Mrs. Stephensen, but I have to ask you some personal questions. Please bear with me. (*Producing a notepad.*) Would you say that you and your husband have a good marriage?

SUSAN: Yes.

COKELY: You're very fortunate. (*He looks at his file.*) In the time you've been married, would you say you and he argue frequently, occasionally, seldom or never?

SUSAN: Occasionally.

COKELY: Occasionally? So you do argue. I thought you said you had a good marriage?

SUSAN: I did. I do.

COKELY: Perhaps "Seldom or Never" would be a more appropriate response for someone with a good marriage. Take as much time as you like to consider the question again.

SUSAN: Thank you. Are you married, Mr. Cokely?

COKELY: No... but I was engaged.

SUSAN: Well, I assure you, it's not uncommon for two people in a good marriage to disagree from time to time. I'll stick with my initial answer.

COKELY: I understand Lt. Blackwood was receiving counseling from the Fleet Chaplain.

SUSAN: (*Slightly stunned.*) Yes.

COKELY: About what?

SUSAN: According to his wife he was having trouble deciding whether or not he was going to stay in the Navy.

COKELY: Perhaps he was talking to the Chaplain about his marriage?

SUSAN: (*Warily.*) Perhaps. How did you know he was speaking with the Fleet Chaplain?

COKELY: (*Ignoring her.*) Now, Mrs. Stephensen, or– may I call you Susan?

SUSAN: (*Reluctantly.*) That's fine.

COKELY: Other than yesterday at Arlington and at the party you and your husband hosted last week, have you spoken with Lt. Lynch in the last several weeks?

SUSAN: Of course, he's our closest friend. He babysat Atticus the day after the party.

COKELY: Lt. Lynch was alone with your little boy?

SUSAN: (*Confused.*) Yes. Atticus is his godchild.

Light change.

SUSAN and COKELY exit.

One week earlier. SUSAN and WILL's quarters. DAN, wearing civilian clothes, silently closes the bedroom door, goes to the table and begins working on a toy airplane. MATT enters wearing his running shorts and a T-shirt, drenched in sweat.

MATT: Dano!

DAN: SHHH! I just got Atticus to sleep.

MATT: Sorry.

MATT peeks in at the baby and then tentatively approaches DAN at the table.

MATT: He's really growing. Does he have his instrument rating yet?

DAN: It wouldn't surprise me.

MATT: He should start walking soon, right?

DAN: Yeah, any day now.

MATT: I meant to call. I had to help Tammi with her Karrie Mae stuff. (*Referring to the plane.*) Attie's gonna go ape-shit over that, Dano.

DAN: It has a life expectancy of less than thirty seconds.

There's an awkward, uncomfortable pause. MATT's really working to get DAN's attention.

MATT: Guess what?

DAN: What?

MATT: (*Genuinely excited.*) I got a call from the detailer this morning... a slot just opened up in the same T.P.S. class you and Will are scheduled for. He's penciled me in. What do you think?

DAN: (*Pause.*) Go for it.

MATT: You think so?

DAN: Absolutely.

MATT: We're gonna set that town on fire!

DAN: Shhh! (*Walking away.*) I'm... changing my orders... asking for Monterey instead.

MATT: Monterey?

DAN: Yeah, foreign language school. I'd like to study Italian.

MATT: But what about Test Pilot School?

DAN: I don't think I want the Space Program anymore.

MATT: What? Since when?

DAN: It's easier for me to get to the islands from this coast anyway. My mom and my brothers– I'd like to get out and see them more.

MATT: You can't save them.

DAN: Hey– they need me okay?

MATT: What am I gonna do?

DAN: Fly your ass off at T.P.S.

MATT: But... I wanted to be in the same class with you
guys.

DAN: Wilbur's gonna be there.

MATT: You. (*Pause.*) I meant you.

DAN: It'd be better if we're separated by a few thousand
miles.

MATT: For whom?

DAN: I watched you shut down again at the party.

MATT: So did you. We were surrounded.

DAN: We're always gonna be surrounded. I'd be best if
I wasn't with you at Pax River.

MATT: (*Suddenly realizing.*) That was your T.P.S. slot, wasn't
it? (*No response.*) That night in Hong Kong I didn't hear
"word one" about you forfeiting your career to take care
of your psycho family. You'd give it all up to be closer to
your folks?

*DAN looks up momentarily. MATT suddenly realizes why
DAN has withdrawn.*

MATT: No... of course not... you changed your orders
because of me.

Walking closer to him.

DAN: Listen, I've been thinking about this a lot... about
you and Tammi... about me and Nance. I want a family
too much. I want stability and respect. I don't want to
jeopardize my career. Hey, we had a drunken night
dancing in a gay disco. Let's just chock it up to
experience. Let's put it behind us. I'm able to do that.
(*He extends his hand.*) What do you say?

MATT: (*Batting his hand away.*) I say that shit doesn't
float! Why are you doing this? I've got your number,
remember?... it's the same as mine.

MATT turns and starts to leave.

DAN: But– What about Tammi?

MATT: (*Stopping and turning.*) She's a lot of those things
I thought I wanted. Things my family wanted me to
want. But I'm not in love with her.

DAN: Don't you want kids... a normal life?

MATT: You know I do! But that's not what's happening here! (*Pause.*) I've made a decision. I want you.

DAN: (*In disbelief.*) But... it's too late... there's... too much to lose.

MATT: Burned, buried or brain dead... until then it's never too late.

Their eyes meet. MATT walks over to DAN and resolutely but tenderly kisses him. After a moment they separate. MATT goes to kiss him again but DAN gently pulls away motioning towards Atticus' room.

DAN: Hey... I– I'm on duty.

MATT: (*Euphoric.*) Yeah. I've gotta shake a leg.

DAN: (*Regaining his senses.*) Hey, aren't you and Wilbur and Boner flying avionics tests this afternoon?

MATT: Jesus! Brain fart. (*Looking at his watch.*) I've gotta shake a leg, I'm scheduled for a 1630 takeoff and I've gotta move my gear aboard the ship before then.

DAN: Move your gear?

MATT: Yeah... Tammi and I split. I'm sleeping on the ship tonight.

DAN: You can stay at my place in the city. I'll be here until late. There's a key above the door.

MATT turns to DAN before exiting.

MATT: Oh yeah, I've been working on this new piece. I've left a cassette in the Stateroom for you... maybe you'll give it a listen... tell me what you think?

DAN: Of course.

MATT: (*He exits, but turns back one last time.*) Oh... above the door?

DAN: (*Smiling.*) Yeah.

MATT exits. DAN lets the airplane fly. It soars. He jumps up and stabs the air with joy.

DAN: YYYYYeeees!

The baby cries. DAN smiles and heads off to his aid.

75

DAN: Comin', Attie!

Crossfade to

The present. SUSAN and WILL's quarters.

COKELY: Were Lt. Lynch and your husband alone together after the party last week?

SUSAN: No... but they've been alone together before. Why?

COKELY: They have?

SUSAN: Of course. (*Growing impatient.*) They were roommates at Annapolis, they share a Stateroom aboard the carrier. What are you implying?

COKELY: I spoke to your husband at his squadron earlier this morning.

SUSAN: Yes?

COKELY: He told me about Lt. Lynch's sexual problem. About his confession yesterday.

SUSAN: (*Hesitatingly.*) He did?

COKELY: I'm here to ascertain if any other officers have engaged in homosexual activity with Lt. Lynch other than Lt. Blackwood.

SUSAN: (*She looks at her watch and stands.*) I'm sorry, Special Agent Cokely, but–

COKELY: "John", please.

SUSAN: This has taken much longer than– I have to feed my son and...

COKELY: I'd like to take you out to lunch there must be someplace nearby...

SUSAN: No. (*Coldly.*) I really have to get on with my day.

COKELY: Did you ever witness sexual relations between Lynch and Blackwood?

SUSAN: This is– they never had that kind of relationship!

COKELY: How do you know?

SUSAN: Because Dan told me. (*Switching gears.*) Mr. Cokely, I thought witch-hunts were a thing of

the past since homosexuality is no longer a crime
in this country...

COKELY: We're not talking about this country, I'm talking
about the laws governing those people in the United
States Navy. Sodomy is a crime under the UCMJ. Please,
Susan, call me John. (*She glares at him.*) Tell me about
your sex life.

SUSAN: That's none of your goddamned business!

COKELY: When I spoke to your husband earlier this
morning, he said you two had argued the night of the
party.

SUSAN: Is this routine for you people? Flying all the way
across the country to harass junior officers and their
wives...?

COKELY: You know, it used to be easy to tell who was
que– gay and who wasn't, but it seems they're getting
better at blending in with the normal people. If I were
a parent, that would give me cause for concern. Now,
how do you know for certain that your hus–

SUSAN: This is ridiculous!

COKELY: Let me remind you, Susan, everything I'm
inquiring about is completely within my purvue as
an investigative agent for the N.I.S.

SUSAN: You've wasted too much of my time asking
highly personal questions to satisfy your own demented
curiosity. (*Regaining her composure.*) Although my husband
and I do argue "occasionally" I think I can say with
reasonable certainty that he has not been sleeping with
Lt. Lynch or any other man.

COKELY: What makes you so sure?

SUSAN: Because I witnessed my husband's reaction
yesterday after the funeral.

Blackout.

*We hear three rifle reports in the black. Then a solo bugle
playing "Taps".*

Scene 5

The previous day. Arlington National Cemetery. WILL and DAN are standing motionless on opposite ends of the stage. DAN is standing downstage staring blankly into space. He's clenching a folded American flag. Both men are silent, consumed with their own thoughts.

WILL: (*Haltingly.*) I... I don't know what happened. It just— I didn't see it coming. I didn't see him.

WILL turns as SUSAN and CHARLIE enter. CHARLIE is wearing his Dress Blues. SUSAN is in a black dress. They separate and CHARLIE moves towards DAN who is still downstage.

WILL: When does our flight leave?

SUSAN: (*Dazed.*) I don't know. (*Pause.*) Yes I do. Five-twenty.

WILL: Did you get us seats next to each other? (*No response.*) Well, that's done.

DAN turns around and faces CHARLIE.

DAN: I'm not sure how I ended up with this. (*Handing him the flag.*) Would you mind giving it to Tammi?

CHARLIE: (*Giving DAN a hug.*) I still can't believe this...

WILL: Why not, it happens all the time. Three aircraft take off. Two aircraft collide. People die. We beat the odds, Boner.

SUSAN: Are you okay, honey?

CHARLIE: (*Through tears.*) I feel so childish for cryin' like this in front of you. Where I come from, you cry and scream and punch walls when someone you love dies. What's wrong with you people?

WILL: You mean you cry! Where you come from people get drunk and shoot other people!

SUSAN: Shut up, Will, he's been through enough.

WILL: Matt's dead. Tears won't bring him back!

CHARLIE: How can you be so fuckin' cold?!

WILL: Whose Navy have you been in for the past four years? Haven't you had other friends crash and burn? Wake up Boner, this ain't Arkansas!

SUSAN: Stop it, Will, please!

WILL: No! I want to know! I can't believe you haven't lost some good friends.

CHARLIE: Not any as close as Matt.

WILL: Well, prepare yourself. I've lost so many I can't even count them.

SUSAN: That's enough, Will.

WILL: I punched out of a mid-air collision with bruises and a bump on the head! Your aircraft wasn't even damaged. Do you have any concept of how lucky we are? Iron Man fucked up and he paid for it... big time. This isn't tiddly-winks in Mr. Rogers' Neighborhood! You've chosen a very dangerous profession, Boner! It blows but it's part of the job. It's just another part of the job!

WILL walks to the opposite side of the stage. SUSAN tries to console CHARLIE.

CHARLIE: (*Trying to compose himself.*) I'd better go see if I can do anything for Tammi and her mom. (*He exits.*)

WILL: Where are Matt's folks?

SUSAN: They left right after the service.

DAN: (*Staring blankly off.*) That's the hardest thing I've ever done.

WILL: It sucked for all of us.

SUSAN: The eulogy was beautiful, Dan.

WILL: There's no way Tammi could have pulled it off. She was hysterical. Have you ever seen so much black eye make-up? She looked like a fucking weeping racoon.

SUSAN: She was upset, Will...

WILL: I heard the comment she made about your dress when we were in the limo... widow or not, you should have kicked her in the twat.

SUSAN: Will, please... this doesn't do anyone any good.

WILL goes to DAN.

WILL: Susan's right, you spoke well, buddy. (*He pats him on the back.*) Well, we'd better get a move on.

WILL and SUSAN begin to exit.

DAN: I won't be going back to Alameda with you tonight.

SUSAN: Why not?

DAN: Two N.I.S. agents approached me before the burial. I think they want to ask me some questions about the accident.

WILL: That's odd.

DAN: (*Beat.*) Do you remember your mother's voice?

SUSAN: What?

WILL: Why'd you ask?

DAN: For a moment there I couldn't remember what Matt's voice sounded like (*Pause.*) I could see him talking and laughing... but I couldn't hear him.

They all reflect on this for a beat.

DAN: I loved Matt.

SUSAN: We all did.

DAN: (*With great difficulty.*) All these years... I've been lying to myself and I didn't even know it.

WILL: What are you talking about, buddy?

DAN: Everywhere I go... everything I see... tells me I'm not supposed to love a man like I loved Matt. That I should never acknowledge it... conceive of it even. But I did. (*He turns to WILL.*) The night I left you in Hong Kong I hadn't forgotten you were waiting. I blew you off. Matt and I were out drinking. We ended up dancing in some club all night. He was hammered... but he was speaking from his heart... and he asked me what I still wanted in life. From somewhere I found the courage to answer truthfully and... I said... "I want you, Matt." He smiled... and said "Ditto." (*Turning away.*) Last week, when I was watching Attie he came by and... we kissed. Just once. But suddenly everything fell into place. And

I knew that I wanted a life with Matt. (*He turns to them.*) The way you two have a life together. And I would have given anything to get it.

WILL and SUSAN are visibly stunned.

DAN: (*Crossing to WILL.*) I'm sorry... I've wanted to tell you.

WILL recoils. He turns blankly to SUSAN.

WILL: We've got to make that flight.

WILL exits. Anguished, torn, SUSAN looks at DAN. Finally, she walks off leaving him alone on stage.

Light changes.

Scene 6

The present. The Stateroom. DAN is moving his things out. He notices somebody has been rifling through his locker. He pulls photos from the back of the locker door and throws them in the trash basket sitting on the desk just as CHARLIE walks in.

DAN: I want to know who went through all of my shit!

CHARLIE: N.I.S.

DAN: N.I.S.? I just spent the last 48 hours with two of their goons... and they still want me back in D.C. by zero-seven-hundred tomorrow morning.

CHARLIE: Did you meet a fella named Cokely?

DAN: (*Stunned.*) Yeah. Why?

CHARLIE: He was here when I returned to the ship yesterday. At first I thought he was a Casualty Assistance Officer collectin' Matt's things for Tammi, but then the questions started.

DAN: (*DAN begins to crumble.*) What questions?

CHARLIE: (*Tentatively.*) One of my workout buddies overheard Cokely talkin' to the Squadron Skipper also. I'm sorry, Dano.

DAN: The Skipper?

DAN sits on his bunk in shock.

CHARLIE: I guess someone reported seein' you in that gay night club.

DAN: (*Lost in thought.*) Jesus...

CHARLIE: Hey, you weren't the only Navy guys there. My workout buddy, the sailor that overheard the N.I.S... I saw him that night too.

DAN: (*Stunned.*) What were you doing there?

CHARLIE: C'mon, Dano, the music's better and the people are more fun. Plus I wanted to party with you and Mattie.

DAN: Why haven't you said anything to me until now?

CHARLIE: I figured it was between you and Iron Man.

DAN finishes packing his bag. CHARLIE goes to the trash can on the desk and fishes out a few 5x7 photographs.

CHARLIE: (*Looking at the prints.*) You sure you wanna throw these out?

DAN: What the hell are you doing?

CHARLIE: (*Looking at another photo and laughing.*) Special Agent Cokely found this one especially titillatin'.

CHARLIE: You remember what we were doing here?

DAN: (*Still Packing.*) No. What?

CHARLIE: Imitatin' "The Creation of Adam". Wilbur was pretendin' he was Moses or somethin' and we were all the angels floatin' around him. (*He studies photo.*) Good thing we weren't created in his image... there'd be a lot of unsatisfied ladies roamin' the planet.

DAN: Deep six 'em...

CHARLIE: C'mon, Dano...

DAN: Trash 'em, Goddammit! (*He throws them on the floor.*)

CHARLIE: It's gonna be lonely out there without you. (*He picks up a picture from the floor.*) Here. (*DAN ignores him.*) Nothin' incriminatin' bout this one. He sure was a handsome dog. (*He looks up at DAN again.*) I'd kinda like to have a picture of Matt.

DAN: Keep it if you like. (*Pause.*) Have you spoken to Wilbur?

CHARLIE: Give it time he'll come around. He's just freaked about the accident.

DAN turns to CHARLIE.

DAN: What really happened up there?

CHARLIE: (*Demonstrating with his hands.*) We were flyin' a tight stacked formation with Wilbur on top, me underneath and Iron Man in the slot. Wilbur called a slow 30 degree roll to the right. I looked up and saw Mattie pull at least a 45 directly up into the belly of Wilbur's plane. Next thing I knew there was fire everywhere. Wasn't till I was back on deck that I learned Wilbur'd punched out of his airplane and that Matt– (*He stops himself.*) What can I do to help you out of this mess?

DAN: Absolutely nothing... unless you wanna go down in flames too. You didn't happen to see a cassette on my bunk or in my desk?

CHARLIE: No.

DAN: Matt was supposed to leave it for me. (*Finding it in his locker.*) Here it is.

As he puts the tape in his pocket, he notices MATT's Cruise Box packed up with all his personal effects. He struggles to suppress his grief.

CHARLIE: What are you gonna do?

DAN: I'm doing fine. Well, I'd better get a move on.

DAN begins to leave. CHARLIE speaks with compassion momentarily stopping him.

CHARLIE: My whole life I've been lookin' for someone. I can't imagine how much you must hurt right now. (*Pause.*) Hey, thanks... for the photo.

DAN: (*Fighting to maintain his composure.*) Fly safe. (*He exits.*)

CHARLIE exits.

Crossfade to

Scene 7

The present. SUSAN and WILL eat their dinner at home in silence. The atmosphere is strained. After several beats SUSAN finally broaches the void.

SUSAN: I went to the base library today.

WILL: Oh?

SUSAN: I was looking for a copy of...

The telephone begins to ring. They both look at each other.

SUSAN: (*Looking at phone.*) Shit. I forgot to turn on the machine. (*To WILL.*) If it's Tammi, I'm not here. I didn't mean that.

WILL: I'm not answering it.

SUSAN: What if it's about your father?

WILL: (*Reluctantly answers phone.*) Hello?

Lights up on DAN on telephone.

DAN: I've spoken to Boner. I know it wasn't your fault. You should know, the N.I.S. has been asking about the Pensacola bird strike. Don't worry, the secret's safe with me. Wilbur, I... I need your–

WILL abruptly hands the phone to SUSAN.

WILL: It's for you.

SUSAN: Hello?

DAN: (*Stunned.*) Hi.

SUSAN: Dano! Where are you?

DAN: I'm at the MAC terminal... headed back to D.C.

SUSAN: Are you okay?

DAN: (*Recovering with false optimism.*) Sure, I'm fine...

SUSAN: Why don't you catch a later flight and stop by the house, I've got enough food–

WILL indicates for her to cut the conversation.

DAN: Susan, I've volunteered for some special duty at the Pentagon.

SUSAN: (*Gingerly.*) Dan– this isn't about special duty. The N.I.S. have threatened us too. They searched the Stateroom... we know they've separated you from the squadron. Why'd you tell them!?

DAN: Me? I didn't...

SUSAN: Who did?

DAN: (*Pause.*) You... and Will.

SUSAN: We did?!

DAN: That's what the N.I.S. told me.

SUSAN realizes what has happened.

SUSAN: Oh, my God! They told us you'd confessed.

DAN: It's too late now.

SUSAN: Will never would have said...

DAN: You could have resisted a little more... played dumb, don't you think?

SUSAN: Don't lay responsibility for this at our feet, Dan. You must have done something to alert them.

DAN: I went dancing in a gay club in Hong Kong.

SUSAN: Dancing? That's considered "Homosexual Behavior"?

DAN: They want a list of names– or they're gonna tell my father.

SUSAN: Who reported this? Don't you have the legal right to challenge your accuser?

DAN: I'm in the Navy. I forfeited my rights years ago.

SUSAN: But this is blackmail! What about your father, or Matt's dad, can't they help?

DAN: Think about it, Susan.

SUSAN: What about Will's dad? He's an Admiral too... he must have some power over the N.I.S... and he loves you... he'll help.

DAN: I'd never ask him to intervene.

SUSAN: Will could ask him. (*She looks at WILL. He turns away.*)

DAN: That's up to Wilbur. (*We hear his flight departure announced.*) Listen, I've got to get on this flight. I know you and Attie will be alone for the next few months. I'll be at the Fort Myer BOQ in Arlington. Call if you need anything.

SUSAN: We'll be fine. I'm worried about you.

DAN: I'm okay. Give Attie a hug for me... Will too.
Gotta go. (*He hangs up.*)

Lights out on DAN. SUSAN hangs up the phone and hands it to WILL hoping he'll call his father. WILL puts it down and goes back to his dinner. SUSAN is stunned.

WILL: So, why'd you go to the library?

SUSAN: To get away. I just sat there for awhile... in the quiet.

WILL: Couldn't you find anything to read?

SUSAN: Will, do you remember the first time we spoke to one another? (*He nods.*) Tenth grade English class... we'd done our term papers on the same book by coincidence.

WILL: "To Kill a Mockingbird".

SUSAN: We were walking home through the woods and I asked you why you'd chosen to report on that book. Do you remember what you said to me?

WILL: I don't really remem–

SUSAN: You said you hoped that one day you could be as good a father as Atticus Finch.

WILL: What does this have to do...?

SUSAN: A white gentleman lawyer defending a black man in the deep south in 1935. Imagine the courage it required to do that? To challenge hundreds of years of racism?

WILL: (*Growing defensive.*) Tom Robinson was convicted and later shot when he tried to escape from jail. It was hardly a victory for Finch.

SUSAN: What was it then?

WILL: (*He gets up from the table.*) Susan, Atticus Finch was an idealist... a fictitious character in a sentimental novel! How about a reality check!

Fadeout.

Scene 8

The present. Dream sequence. We hear MATT's music (Pat Metheny's Secret Story: "Not to be forgotten") throughout. A blue light comes up on MATT, stage left. After a few moments, another light comes up on DAN asleep in a chair, obviously dreaming. He awakens and searches for the source of the music. He turns to find MATT.

DAN: (*Joyfully.*) I knew it... I knew you got out of that plane!

MATT turns to DAN and puts his index finger to his mouth signaling for DAN to be quiet. The music continues as MATT listens intently and begins to gently conduct. DAN slowly walks toward MATT. As he tries to rest his head in MATT's outstretched hand we hear a knocking which causes MATT to drop his hand and look in the direction of the sound before DAN can touch him. Just as DAN is about to take MATT's hand, we hear another knock and MATT disappears into the dark. DAN backs up into the chair. We hear the knocking again.

Lights up.

DAN's BOQ room in Arlington. DAN is asleep in the chair stage right. A tape player plays MATT's music. There is a knock at the door.

SUSAN: Dan?

DAN: (*Disoriented he jerks awake.*) What–? Who is it?

SUSAN: Dano, it's Susan!

DAN turns off the tape player and holds the cassette in his hand. SUSAN enters wearing a winter coat.

DAN: (*Still disoriented.*) What time is it? (*He looks for his watch.*)

SUSAN: It's late.

DAN: Are you okay?

Shaken from the vividness of the dream, he is unable to look at her.

SUSAN: I'm fine.

DAN: Will! Is he okay?

87

SUSAN: He's fine...

DAN: What about Attie? Why are you in D.C.?

SUSAN: Fine. He's at home. Will's dad had another heart attack.

DAN: Oh... no.

SUSAN: Are you alright?

DAN: *(Moving away.)* I'm fine. I just flew in from Honolulu a couple of hours ago. They gave me a few days leave to go see my folks. Can I get you some water, that's about all–

SUSAN: No– thanks. How are your parents?

DAN: My dad left in the middle of his own party– had to go to the office. My mom was drunk... so were most of the guests. I had about ten minutes alone with her the next morning. The entire time she was dressing for an Officers' Wives Club luncheon.

SUSAN: Is she still pretending everything's fine?

DAN: She's under the impression I'm here on Temporary Duty because I've developed a fear of flying or something... she doesn't wanna know the real reason. "It's probably just a phase", she said. I asked her if she should be taking so many Valium and she said "Look, they come in a new color don't you just love this shade of pale yellow?"

SUSAN: Poor thing. *(Pause.)* Do you think it could be a phase?

DAN: Can a phase last a lifetime? You know her... she's been out of it like this for as long as...

SUSAN: I meant *you*– Your attraction to– Could it be a phase?

DAN: *(Beat.)* No, Susan. It's not a phase. Is that why you stopped by at three a.m.? *(No response.)* Is it?

SUSAN: *(Gravely.)* The N.I.S. called yesterday. They said you've implicated Will. They want names or they'll haul him off the ship for more questioning and say that he's–

DAN: It's a lie! They're bluffing. The N.I.S. can't prove that I did anything but dance in a gay club. Next they'll say I sabotaged Matt's aircraft because he rebuffed my advances.

SUSAN: Stop!

DAN: Matt had more than 2500 hours in the 18... I've replayed every moment of that day... something *I* might have said or done that...

SUSAN: (*Firmly.*) Dan– *It was an accident!* Everyone makes mistakes... even you guys. (*Beat.*) Have you spoken to Nancy?

DAN: She's left several messages. I haven't returned them.

SUSAN: I thought you really cared about her.

DAN: I do.

SUSAN: She's still in love with you, you know.

DAN: I think you're right. It's late.

SUSAN: I'm sorry...

DAN: I can't believe I'm hearing you say this.

SUSAN: What? I don't understand...

DAN: No. You don't.

SUSAN: It's just that– I have a lot of questions...

DAN: So do I.

SUSAN: We all knew you couldn't be– maybe this *is* just a temporary thing.

DAN: No.

SUSAN: How do you know?

DAN: How do you know you're heterosexual?

SUSAN: When did you realize it?

DAN: A few months ago.

SUSAN: You mean you just woke up one morning and you were–?

DAN: Yes. I went to put on my black uniform shoes and I thought to myself (*Beat.*) I'd look much better in these if they had a six-inch stiletto heel.

SUSAN: (*Tenuously.*) Really? (*He begins to laugh.*) I can't
believe you're laughing. Your career's on the line. I'm
serious, Dan.

DAN: It was a process. Listening to myself.

SUSAN: (*Pause.*) So your relationship with Nancy was a
cover-up?

DAN: No. (*Frustrated.*) I loved her very much. I still do.

SUSAN: Then why can't you two–? Dan– just call her! The
N.I.S. will see you're with a woman and leave you alone!

DAN: Do you have any idea how much energy I've wasted
trying to feed this lie? The countless nights
we settled for less trying to make it work? (*SUSAN is
silent.*) What I feel is not sick, or queer, or perverted!

SUSAN: Dan... we never said that.

DAN: Exactly! You said nothing! You and Wilbur and
my parents and the whole fucking world... including
myself, *assumed* I wanted everything you wanted! Well,
we were wrong. Dead wrong! (*Grabbing her wrists.*)
Susan– I was *in love* with Matt!

We see a sudden epiphany in her face.

DAN: Now, in less than four hours, I'm meeting the N.I.S.
for my sixteenth interrogation session. I need some sleep.

SUSAN: (*In tears.*) Oh, my God... I'm sorry... I'm so sorry!
(*She exits.*)

*For several moments he stares blankly into space before turning
on the tape player again. He listens to the music. It swells. In
a fit of rage he kicks the tape player violently until the music
stops. Exhausted, he stands in a stupor before giving in to sobs
of grief.*
Slow fade.

Scene 9

*The present. Dream Sequence. The Stateroom. WILL is asleep
in his bunk. We hear music (Pat Metheny's Secret Story: "The
Truth Will Always be") in the background. We hear MATT's
voice from offstage.*

We hear the whine of an aircraft going down. It grows increasingly loud over the music.

MATT: Wilbur... Wilbur? I'm going down! I'm going down!

WILL: Matt... Matt? Mattie!

MATT: You hit the Mockingbirds!

WILL: I didn't see them. I didn't see the birds.

CHARLIE enters the Stateroom wearing his flight suit.

WILL: Don't go! Please don't go! Mattieeeeee?!!

The sound is deafening. WILL sits up in his bunk screaming. CHARLIE turns on the lights.

CHARLIE: (*Grabbing WILL by the shoulders.*) You okay, buddy?

WILL: (*Covering his eyes.*) Cut the lights!

CHARLIE: What?

WILL: The lights! Cut the freakin' lights! (*Putting on his sunglasses; shaken.*) What time is it?

CHARLIE: Twenty thirty-five... you sure you're okay?

WILL: (*Jumping up.*) I gotta get my ass in gear. I brief in ten minutes.

CHARLIE: Brief? You must have really been out. They've gotta do some work on the electrical system. We're makin' a beeline for the Subic Bay shipyards. Liberty at last!

WILL: Fuck Subic, the place is a hell hole.

CHARLIE: Hell hole or not right now I don't care. We've been on station flyin' our asses to the bone for 5 weeks straight... I'm ready for some down time. Ding-Ding. Mail call. (*He hands him a letter.*) From Susan.

CHARLIE sees a picture of MATT on the back of WILL's locker door.

CHARLIE: Guess you found the print Dano gave me. Iron Man was lookin' rather studly here, don't you think?

WILL: (*Ignoring CHARLIE, he opens the letter.*) She's volunteering two days a week at the Naval Hospital...

they're paying her for a third day. (*Reading the letter.*) "Please give my love to Charlie and tell him to double bag that thing when you stop in Subic Bay."

CHARLIE: No way, she didn't write that...

WILL: Swear to God! Look. (*Handing letter to CHARLIE.*)

CHARLIE takes the letter, reads it aloud and laughs. WILL takes it back.

CHARLIE: Anything about your Daddy?

WILL: She says he's not so well. He's a tough bird though, he'll outlive us all.

CHARLIE: Hope so. I've been missin' them a lot lately. (*No response from WILL.*) You miss Iron Man don't you?

WILL: I don't think about it. It'll fuck with your head.

CHARLIE: What about Dano? Don't you miss him?

WILL looks as if he's going to break down. He refuses to acknowledge his grief.

WILL: (*Paraphrasing SUSAN's letter.*) Apparently Tammi's moved back to Selma with her mother. Susan said she left town in a brand new BMW convertible... black... I guess that's a good look for a Navy widow.

CHARLIE: I hope she finds what she's lookin' for.

WILL: I think she has.

CHARLIE: You might not like what she's gotta say but at least she says it... she's an open book. Bigger balls than a Texas Longhorn.

WILL continues reading the letter.

CHARLIE: I didn't figure you'd be so uptight about this whole thing... about Dano.

WILL: I don't want to– listen, this is between him and me! Period. End of story.

CHARLIE: Not so. This has nothin' to do with him it's been all about you.

WILL: I don't understand him, okay, let's drop it!

CHARLIE: Wilbur... the scuttlebutt is the guy that ratted on Dano has just identified himself to the N.I.S. You guys have been best friends forever, why can't you–?

WILL: He lied!

CHARLIE: To himself! You wanna tell me about the sunglasses, Wilbur? (*No response.*) Nah... I didn't think so.
WILL removes his sunglasses. He looks cornered. CHARLIE softens.

CHARLIE: It's not like he opened fire on a nursin' home or somethin'. (*Silence.*) Hell, I had a couple of experiences with guys a few years back... had to be sure I wasn't missin' anything.

WILL: Why am I not surprised?

CHARLIE: I don't understand why everybody starts twistin' off and quotin' dead prophets when two people of the same sex wanna touch each other. The enemy isn't somewhere over *there*! (*Pointing to his head.*) It's here... (*Pointing to his heart.*) and here. By allowin' fag jokes to circulate the wardroom without speakin' out against it... we became their enemies.
They both contemplate this for a moment.

WILL: So what was the verdict?

CHARLIE: About what?

WILL: Sex with guys. Have we been missing anything?

CHARLIE: I can only speak for myself. Remember I told you about my cousin, Larry? Best damn B.J. I ever got. Boy he could honk on Bobo's nose.

WILL: So why didn't you switch permanently?

CHARLIE: Cuz I'm kinda partial to burying my face in a pair of 38 Ds.
WILL contemplates this.

CHARLIE: What difference does it make? He's the same person he's always been... he's your buddy and you need to be able to love him. (*Pause.*) At least he's stayin' within his own species.

WILL: You know you can get syphilis that way.

CHARLIE: (*He shakes his head.*) We used Glad Bags. You think the Pope would approve of condoms under those circumstances?

WILL walks over to his locker and looks at the picture. CHARLIE's demeanor is suddenly grave. He seems as if he might shatter into pieces.

CHARLIE: Wilbur?

WILL: Yeah?

CHARLIE: I think Iron Man's dead cuz of me.

WILL: What the hell are you talking about?

CHARLIE: That afternoon... before our flights...
I overheard the Skipper tellin' Matt he'd heard a rumor that he'd gone to a gay club in Hong Kong... and that if it were true it might severely affect his consideration for T.P.S. Of course Matt sounded convincin' denyin' it but when he walked out of that office, he looked white as a ghost. I should've canceled the flight... he was too distracted... his head wasn't in the cockpit.

WILL: And there's nothing anyone could've done about it!
His ability to compartmentalize went out the window.
He took his private life into the aircraft! Hell, he could've killed us both. He ate it and it's nobody's fault but his own.

CHARLIE: Dano needs your help, Will–

WILL: Hey! I've got a family to support! I can't be worried about whether or not Dan Lynch is getting a fair shake.
You play, you pay... them's the breaks of Naval Air!
They're both quiet for several beats. CHARLIE stares at WILL in disbelief.

WILL: What?

CHARLIE: Nothin'. At least nothin' you'd notice. I've gotta get topside... it's cold as hell in this room. (*He exits.*)
Blackout.

Scene 10

The present. The Pentagon Interrogation Room. COKELY smokes furiously as he compares some files to one another. JONES is sitting.

JONES: You've been starin' at those medical records for five weeks now there's nothing there. Your shootin' at shadows, John. He's denied everything except going to that gay bar. That's it! Stephensen and his wife will probably deny they let on to anything at all if questioned again. Why don't you just give up on this guy he's not—

COKELY: BINGO! (*He refers to another page and smiles.*)

JONES: What?

COKELY: Got 'im! I've got him now!

JONES: What are you—?

COKELY: My informant has prepared a statement verifying that he saw Lynch engaged in a homosexual act. With that and this additional evidence, I'm gonna nail this snot-nosed Lieutenant and force him to expose every fudge-packin' son-of-a-...

JONES: John, we've got dozens of other cases to get to! You're not gonna get Lynch to squeal on his friends! Give it up!

COKELY: So the rest of us should have to live with a fucked up, less effective system because of the few freaks that want to stir the pot? Do you know what these guys do? Do you? (*JONES doesn't respond.*) They stick soda bottles and rodents up each other's asses! It's true! They parade around in dresses and leather pants with their cocks hanging out! They take all kinds of drugs— they put earrings in their tits. They completely abuse their bodies. This is good for the military? This is good for the country? Too many people have worked too hard! I want every last homo out.

JONES: And I'm a spear-chuckin' nigger, right?

COKELY doesn't respond.

JONES: I'm gonna bring him in here and he's gonna sign a statement affirming that he visited a homosexual establishment... period. The letter will go into his record and probably kill his career anyway. That's all we can nail him on. Let's end this thing now and send him back to his squadron where he belongs. Okay?

COKELY continues to ignore JONES.

JONES: Crucifying an Admiral's kid isn't gonna change the fact that you grew up the son of an Enlisted Man!

COKELY: (*Exposed, he wheels around.*) What!?

JONES: Your daddy wasn't an Officer... (*Holding up a file.*) We've all got a record, John.

JONES steps stage left and yells.

JONES: Dan!

DAN enters wearing Dress Blues. JONES motions for him to sit. He sits.

COKELY: Seems like you fly-boys spend all your spare time burying friends and family. Tell you what, if you help me, I'll think about giving you Wednesday off so you can attend the "festivities" over at the cemetery. So, did you remember any names over the weekend?

JONES: John?

DAN: I went dancing in a gay discotheque. That's it.

COKELY: (*He waves the records.*) You're smart enough to know that in my hand I have your complete Service Jacket, Fitness Reports, Medical Records... Accident Report.

JONES: Jesus, John–

COKELY: (*Consulting the records.*) We've got a flight surgeon connected with the N.I.S. that suggested we give you and Stephensen another exam to determine if you've been lying to us.

DAN: (*Thinking COKELY's found out about the bail out coverup.*) I don't understand.

COKELY: After close scrutiny of the Accident Report from your Pensacola mishap...

JONES: John!

COKELY: I came across some information that proves you and your buddy have been hiding something from us... for the past five years. (*Pause.*) Your "friend", Will, has signed an affidavit.

DAN: That's horseshit!

COKELY: Is it? Is it, Dan!?

DAN and COKELY engage in a standoff for several beats.
DAN looks terrified.

JONES: (*To COKELY.*) Come on, John! (*He puts a document in front of DAN.*) Sign this so we can all go home.

COKELY takes the paper from DAN and wads it up.

JONES: What the hell are you doing!?

COKELY: According to the post accident medical exam, Lt. Stephensen and Lt. Ivey here were both complaining of hemorrhoids after they ditched that plane in the bay. (*To JONES.*) What do you think those two boys did all night before the rescue team found them?

JONES: What the hell are you talkin' about?

COKELY: Proof! That he likes bending over for his buddies!

JONES: They pull high G's in tactical aircraft, John. Jet jocks get hemorrhoids!

COKELY: (*To DAN.*) Your buddy, Wilbur, sang like a canary for me...

JONES: You've taken this too far, John!

COKELY: Shut the fuck up! This is still my case. (*Sneering at JONES.*) Seems like you've made a friend, Lieutenant. (*To DAN.*) I've got space here for five names, you just reel 'em off and I'll write 'em down... you won't even have to lift your pen. Danny?

DAN refuses to be drawn in.

COKELY: I'll start the ball rolling. (*He writes.*) Blackwood... Matthew... W...

DAN bolts out of his chair and tries to grab the clipboard from COKELY.

DAN: Go fuck yourself!

COKELY: Maybe you could show me how.

JONES: John! You're way out of line!

DAN: Contrary to what you want to believe, I'm not interested in dressing like a woman, marching in parades or, least of all, showing you how to fuck yourself! I am not a professional "gay". I am a professional Naval Officer. I refuse to be defined by my sexuality.

COKELY: You can refuse until you rot, Lieutenant.
(*He takes a tape recorder from his coat pocket and plays back*
"... I refuse to be defined by my sexuality".) That last
statement was as much as I need. I own your ass.
Simple as that.

DAN: Special Agent Cokely, you don't own me. (*He
takes an envelope from his breast pocket and thrusts it
at COKELY.*) My resignation. Check Mate. (*He turns
to JONES.*) Special Agent Jones, have a good day.
DAN exits.
Crossfade to

Scene 11

*The present. A hotel room in Arlington, Virginia. SUSAN and
WILL have just returned from WILL's father's funeral. WILL
holds a folded American flag downstage while SUSAN packs.*

WILL: There were so many times I wanted to ask Dad
if he'd had it to do all over again... would he have left
Nebraska... would he have ever left Grandpa's farm.

SUSAN: Why didn't you?

WILL: He was always gone... out at sea.

SUSAN: Not for the last few years.

WILL: It's a moot point now.

SUSAN: Moot? (*Trying to contain her anger.*) You've been
racing around the sky for the past seven years risking
your life day and night. For what? The preservation
of freedom? What freedom? (*He doesn't respond.*) The
evening of the accident when the Casualty Assistance
Officer pulled up in front of our quarters... I began
to panic. All I could see was burning wreckage... and
your face. But then he asked me for directions to
Quarters twenty-three and I felt the most incredible
wave of relief... as if God really understood my potential
grief and had granted me yet another reprieve. Atticus
and I had been spared again. And as I watched him
continue driving down the street in his shiny black

sedan, I realized Matt and Tammi lived in twenty-three... and I ran inside to tell Dano what had happened.

WILL: I wish you wouldn't worry...

SUSAN: These past weeks I dreamed the same dream night after night. A Casualty Assistance Officer would somberly walk up to our front door and tell me you were lost at sea and I'd fall to the ground unable to control my sobbing.

WILL: I'm a good pilot. Nothing's gonna happen to me.

SUSAN: Until last night. It was the same dream... but this time when the officer told me you were missing... instead of falling apart... I felt no pain. I felt... relief.

WILL is silent. SUSAN moves to the other side of the room.

SUSAN: Why didn't you cry today?

WILL: What?

SUSAN: You didn't shed one tear. (*WILL turns away from her.*) Why not?

WILL: Please, Susan...

SUSAN: The Honor Guard just buried your last relative in Arlington. Didn't that crush you?

WILL: Of course.

SUSAN: You must feel something. Don't you? (*No response.*) Why didn't you cry?

WILL: I have my own way of grieving.

SUSAN: It's called not feeling. What's happened to you? You've turned into an automaton.

WILL: (*Walking to the suitcase and placing the flag in it.*) I'm so sick of this "sensitive man" crap! Not every guy has to cry to–! You've been listening to Boner too much. Where would this country be if we all fell apart every time someone died? It's part of my job to hold it together.

SUSAN: Bullshit! Why didn't you cry!?

WILL: Because! I didn't feel anything! (*He begins to exit.*) I'm going to pay the bill, please be ready to leave when I return.

There's a knock on the hotel door just as WILL opens it.

WILL: Yes!

DAN stands in the doorway with a package in his hand. Unable to look him in the eye, WILL quickly turns and walks downstage. SUSAN goes to the door.

DAN: Sorry to disturb you but I wanted to catch you before you left. I– I've been thinking about you... about your dad... since I heard. He was a good man. I'm sorry. (*He hands her an envelope with a bow on it.*) This is for Attie... his birthday.

SUSAN: Oh, Dan, that's so thoughtful of you.

DAN: It's one of my photos. Not your typical present for a one-year-old. But I figured...

SUSAN: Can you come in for awhile?

WILL: Susan, we really have to get moving. Our flight leaves soon.

DAN: Thanks anyway but...

SUSAN: (*To WILL but watching DAN.*) We've got time, honey– I have to go down to the lobby for a minute. Why don't you two talk.

WILL: You don't need anything in the lobby! Susan! We have to be at the airport in less than thirty minutes.

DAN: How can we talk? He can't even look at me.

SUSAN: Sure he can. (*To WILL.*) I'll be back in a little–

WILL: You're going nowhere, Susan! We have to be on that flight!

DAN: He can't. (*To SUSAN.*) He can't even look at me. (*To WILL.*) Can you?! (*WILL won't respond. To SUSAN.*) Matt died six weeks ago and I haven't heard one word from your husband. I would've gone to the ends of the earth for him... and I thought he would've for me. Please give the photo to Attie.

He starts to go and then turns one last time. WILL still refuses to look at him.

DAN: It must make your skin crawl to think that at one time

you and I were best friends. Six weeks and not one word. Not one... fucking... word.

Walking to within inches of WILL's face.

DAN: Last chance, buddy. Come on, say it. I know you want to. Say it. Say it. Say it you fucking coward!

WILL: (*Exploding.*) Faggot!!

WILL hits DAN in the chest. They struggle. Within seconds DAN has WILL in a head-lock and forces him to the floor. DAN lets go of WILL, gets up and heads for the door. SUSAN blocks DAN's exit with her body.

DAN: Let me go, there's nothing more to say...

SUSAN: Will!? Please! Talk to him!

WILL gets up, grabs the flag and hurls it at DAN's feet. SUSAN moves out of the way to the corner of the room.

WILL: Fuck you! I'm the guy that's always been there! I'm your best buddy!

DAN: Then where the hell have you been!? I've been harassed and silenced and humiliated, my career's in the shit-can and there's not a single person I can turn to! What the fuck are you moaning about!? What the fuck have you lost!?

WILL: Youuuuu! (*Unable to look at DAN.*) When you told me you were in love with Matt I didn't know where I fit into your life. Why wasn't our friendship enough? I thought– I thought I was the man you loved the most. You can screw women... you can screw men... I don't give a damn who you fuck... it doesn't matter! (*He starts to crumble.*) But where do I fit in now? What happens to me?

DAN is speechless. WILL continues after a few beats.

WILL: It was my fault. I called it. I called the slow right roll... he pulled up into the belly of my plane...

DAN: You couldn't get out of the way. It happened too fast.

WILL: I should have seen him.

DAN: No– he was underneath you– you couldn't have seen him!

WILL: His airplane exploded. In two seconds it was over. There was nothing left of him. Three days later we were burying an empty casket and– I tried to tell you about it... before you told us... how you loved him. And then Boner and I were out at sea again... and I tried to forget about Matt. About all of them... but I couldn't. I started to count. I couldn't stop counting. And just when I thought I'd finished– I'd remember another. (*He cracks more.*) How many buddies have we lost?

DAN: (*Quietly.*) I don't know.

WILL: Twelve! Twelve guys– including Mattie– just gone... and for what!? (*Weeping.*) If you don't crash and burn you could die from that fucking disease. Who can beat those odds?

Long silence.

WILL: I thought– what about all our plans... our kids?

DAN: I tried so hard to stop it. Things changed.

WILL: I don't know what to do– where to begin. All that work– everything– just down the tubes. Who the hell am I gonna serve with? What about T.P.S.?

DAN: I don't know.

WILL: I'll threaten my resignation if they don't drop the charges... is that what you want?

DAN: Threaten the Commander in Chief? No.

WILL: There must be a way to change this. There's gotta be a way!

DAN: No, it's too late. (*With resolve.*) I won't hide anymore. No more lies.

WILL sobs. We hear Pat Metheny's "Tell Her You Saw Me" very quietly under the scene.

SUSAN: Is this the photo Agent Cokely got such a charge out of?

DAN: No, I don't think Attie's quite ready for that one.

She takes DAN's photo out of the envelope. It's a picture of the four men together. She looks at it and takes it over to WILL. He sobs.

SUSAN: (*After several beats she looks at WILL.*) Can we start over? (*To DAN.*) All of us?

DAN: (*DAN picks up the flag at his feet.*) I don't know.

WILL: What do you want me to say?

DAN: Say anything. Ask me anything. Just don't stop talking to me.

Nobody moves. After several beats WILL looks up and finally looks directly at DAN. A beat. WILL places a hand on SUSAN's shoulder. Perhaps the wall between them has begun to crumble.

Fadeout. End.